# Contents

# How to Use Ten-Minute Activities

**Keep *Ten-Minute Activities* handy.**

* Choose an activity for each subject area—language arts, mathematics, social studies, science, and indoor recess—that is appropriate to the skill level of your students.
* Mark these pages with sticky notes.
* Read through each activity to make sure you understand the steps.
* Gather any materials that must be prepared in advance, label them with the activity name and page number, and set them aside.
* After you use an activity, immediately choose and prepare another in that subject area so that you always have five activities ready to go.

Although these short activities do not require teaching a lesson to execute, it is always best to plan ahead just as you would for a lesson in any subject.

For activities done in small groups, you can save time if groups are designated in advance. If you seat your students in clusters of desks or tables, you may, of course, use seating as the group designator. Or you may prepare and post a chart of partners and groups. Be sure to include the location that each group is to meet. When the need for a 10-minute activity arises, you need only say, "Gather with your group."

# Poster Play

by Delana Heidrich

▶ **Materials:** posters or large pictures, paper, pencils

▶ **Here's How!**

1. In advance, gather a collection of posters or large pictures. (Calendar pictures work well.)

2. Display one picture at a time.

3. Tell students that they have 30 seconds to write a title for the poster or picture that clearly expresses what it is about.

4. After 30 seconds, remove the picture and show the next one.

5. After students have written the titles for four or five pictures, allow time for sharing. For maximum participation, show the first picture again. Students read their title to a neighbor. Then have some titles shared with the whole class. Be sure to discuss the elements that make a good title for each picture.

# Headliners

### by Kathy Mattenklodt

▶ **Materials:** front page of newspaper, paper, pencils (optional)

▶ **Here's How!**

1. Show the front page of the local newspaper.

2. Discuss how headlines must tell in a very few words what a story is all about—to express the main idea of the story.

3. Display another picture found in the newspaper.

4. Have students tell or write a headline to go with the picture.

# The Same Game

by Laurie Williams

▶ **Materials:** none

▶ **Here's How!**

1. Choose three students who have something in common (long hair, blue jeans, only children, braces, missing tooth, flowers in clothing, glasses, etc.) to stand in the front of the room.

2. Other students in the class guess what all three students have in common by asking the teacher only questions with a *Yes* or *No* answer. The object is to be the first student to guess the similarity correctly.

3. The student who guesses correctly chooses three more students who have a trait in common and answers *Yes* and *No* to the questions posed.

**Example**

Brian, Hannah, and Debbie are chosen to stand in the front because they all have one shoelace untied. The dialogue might proceed as follows:

| | |
|---|---|
| Student #1: | Does the similarity have to do with clothing? |
| Teacher: | YES |
| Student #2: | Is the similarity something on their backs? |
| Teacher: | NO |
| Student #3: | Is the similarity that they all have on pants? |
| Teacher: | They do all have on pants, but NO, that's not it. |
| Student #4: | Is the similarity above the waist? |
| Teacher: | NO |
| Student #5: | Is the similarity that they all have shoes on? |
| Teacher: | NO |
| Student #6: | Is it that they all have at least one shoe untied? |
| Teacher: | YES!! Now you get to pick three students. |

# Being Brief

by Delana Heidrich

▶ **Materials:** paper, pencils

▶ **Here's How!**

1. Divide students into three groups.

2. Give each group a different assignment:

   • Group 1 must write five bumper sticker slogans pertaining to school or education. Each slogan must consist of 10 or fewer words.

   • Group 2 must write five favorable fortune cookie sayings about school or education, each consisting of no more than 10 words.

   • Group 3 must write five button slogans advertising their own school or the value of education in general. The buttons must consist of six words or less.

3. After each group has completed its assignment, allow its members to share the group's results with the rest of the class. Discuss the difficulties in keeping comments brief, yet complete.

▶ **Variation**

Require all students to complete one of the activities described instead of breaking your class into groups.

bumper stickers

School Is Cool!

Your grades are on the way up!

fortune cookies

buttons

Bay View is Tops

# Small Talk

by Delana Heidrich

▶ **Materials:** paper, pencils

▶ **Here's How!**

1. Explain to students that a single topic can be covered in few or in many words.

2. Describe for your class the following scenario:

   > You are on vacation in Mexico having a good time when you realize you forgot to tell your grandma you were going. You decide you'd better inform her of your trip. Unfortunately, Grandma has no phone.

3. Instruct each student to send his or her grandmother a telegram telling her the news. Tell students they are charged for each word they use and can only afford to include five words.

4. Allow up to 2 minutes for writing.

5. Now instruct each of your students to write a postcard to Grandma telling her about the vacation. Thirty words will fit on the postcard.

6. Allow up to 4 minutes for writing.

▶ **Variation**

Choose a topic from any subject area that the students have studied. Require students to write about the topic in one sentence, four sentences, and then in a paragraph. Although details will become more complex with each assignment, the main idea should come through in all of the writings.

# Is That a Fact?

by Martha Cheney

▶ **Materials:** assorted small objects in a box or bag

▶ **Here's How!**

1. Select an object and show it to the students. For example, the object might be a fuzzy toy rabbit.

2. Call on a student and ask him or her to state a **fact** about the object, such as, "The rabbit has two ears."

3. Ask another student to state an **opinion**, such as, "The rabbit is cute."

4. Require students to express their answers in complete sentences.

5. Allow the group to determine whether the statement given is indeed a fact or an opinion by giving a "thumbs up" or "thumbs down" signal.

▶ **Variation**

Ask students to write one fact and one opinion about the object.

# Who Am I?

by Delana Heidrich

▶ **Materials:** none

▶ **Here's How!**

1. Select one student to be IT. IT describes a character from a well-known book, story, or nursery rhyme in a single sentence (e.g., *This character eats little piggies*).

2. IT then selects a student to guess the character who was described. If the student guesses the character correctly, he or she becomes IT.

   If the student cannot guess the character described, IT gives another one-sentence clue.

3. IT continues to provide one-sentence clues until someone guesses the described character.

▶ **Variation**

Students describe famous people from history or current culture.

This character eats little piggies...

# What's in a Name?

by Kathy Mattenklodt

▶ **Materials:** paper, pencils (optional)

▶ **Here's How!**

1. Think of the first name of a character in a story with which students are familiar (e.g., James, Henry, Cinderella).

2. Give clues to the name of the character. These can be personal attributes, spelling clues, or a combination of both. You may want students to record the clues.

3. Students guess the name of the character.

▶ **Variation**

Use names of students in the class to classify attributes and aid in team building.

# Book Review

by Martha Cheney

▶ **Materials:** a few good books

▶ **Here's How!**

This is a quick way to whet your students' appetites for quality books. Keep a selection of your favorite titles in a handy location in the classroom. Choose one to share with students.

1. Tell a little bit about the book and/or the author.

2. Describe the setting or give an intriguing fact about the main character.

3. Read the first few paragraphs aloud if you have time.

▶ **Variation**

After you have modeled this process a few times, invite students to give "reviews" of books they have enjoyed reading.

# Context Clues
by Kathy Mattenklodt

▶ **Materials:** list of age-appropriate vocabulary words, chart paper or overhead transparency, paper, pencils (optional)

▶ **Here's How!**

1. In advance, prepare a list of age-appropriate vocabulary words that students are not likely to know. The words may be taken from reading or content studies.

2. Point to a word, pronounce it, and use it in a sentence. The sentence must provide sufficient clues as to the meaning of the word.

**Examples**
Not enough clues
   The **clamorous** students ran out the door.
Enough clues
   The **clamorous** students yelled, screamed, and ran out the door.

Not enough clues
   I think the story is **fictitious**.
Enough clues
   I think the story is **fictitious** because a peach couldn't grow that big.

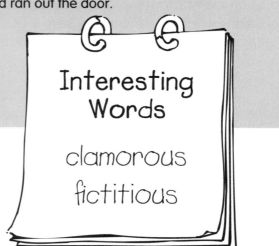

Interesting Words

clamorous

fictitious

3. Have students write a definition or discuss possible definitions with a partner.

4. Share responses.

# Rhyme Time

by Tekla White

▶ **Materials:** none

▶ **Here's How!**

1. Divide the class into two teams. One student on each team is the team captain. The captain selects the person on the team who will give the answer.

2. The Team 1 captain chooses someone on the team to name a one-syllable word.

3. Team 2 receives a point if they can give a rhyming word. The team should confer first and agree on the answer; the captain designates the team member to provide the answer.

4. Team 2 challenges Team 1 with a new one-syllable word, and Team 1 tries to come up with a rhyming word.

▶ **Variation**

Play the game with two-syllable words.

# Opposites
### by Tekla White

▶ **Materials:** chalkboard, chalk, paper, pencils

▶ **Here's How!**

1. Divide the class into teams. Each team needs paper and a pencil.

2. Each team writes a pair of antonyms on its paper.

3. Then the first team writes one of its antonyms on the board.

4. Each of the other teams has an opportunity to give an antonym for the one on the board.

   * Award a point for any correct antonym.

   * The team that wrote the word on the board may give its antonym last to earn a point if no other team gave it.

   * Antonyms can't be repeated.

5. The next team writes one of its antonyms on the board and the game continues.

---

**Example**

The first team writes *tiny* and *large* on their paper. A team member writes *tiny* on the board. The other teams might give the antonyms *huge*, *enormous*, and *gigantic*. The team that wrote *tiny* on the board can then earn a point by saying *large* because the other teams didn't use that antonym.

---

▶ **Variation**

The teams write pairs of synonyms instead of antonyms.

# ABCs of *Said*
### by Kathy Mattenklodt

▶ **Materials:** paper, pencils, dictionaries (optional)

▶ **Here's How!**

1. Divide students into groups of four.

2. Tell students that you get tired of reading sentences and stories with the word *said* used over and over. Point out that there is a multitude of more descriptive words that could be used instead of *said*.

3. Each group of students chooses a recorder who writes the letters of the alphabet down the side of the group's paper.

4. For each letter, challenge groups to write a word that could be used in place of *said*.

## ABCs of *SAID*

| | |
|---|---|
| A–answered | M–murmured |
| B–bellowed | N–noted |
| C–called | O–objected |
| D–declared | P–piped up |
| E–exclaimed | Q–quipped |
| F–faltered | R–remarked |
| G–growled | S–stated |
| H–harangued | T–teased |
| I–insisted | U–uttered |
| J–jabbered | V–vowed |
| L–lamented | W–whined |
| | Y–yelled |

5. Allow groups 5 minutes to fill in as many words as they can. (Allow the use of dictionaries if you wish.)

6. In another session, compile group lists into a large class list. Post the list for students to refer to when writing.

# Adjective Adventure

by Kathy Mattenklodt

▶ **Materials:** chalkboard, chalk, paper, pencils

▶ **Here's How!**

1. Pick a noun and write it on the chalkboard.

2. Have students write the noun and then write an adjective that describes the noun. The adjective must begin with the **last** letter of the noun.

3. Add another adjective. It must begin with the **last** letter of the first adjective.

4. Continue adding adjectives. Each new adjective must begin with the **last** letter of the previous adjective.

5. Have students share their lists with the class.

**Examples**
motorcycle—eye-catching, green, new, wondrous, speedy
river—rapid, deep, powerful, long, glimmering
kid—dynamic, clever, resourceful, lucky

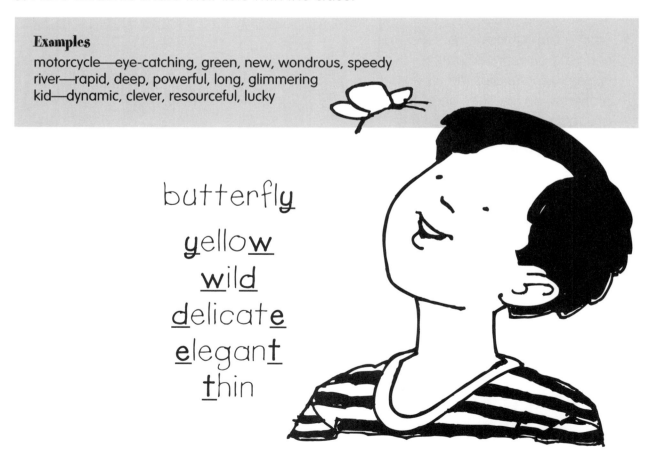

butterfly
yellow
wild
delicate
elegant
thin

# Awesome Alliterations

by Kathy Mattenklodt

▶ **Materials:** paper, pencils

▶ **Here's How!**

1. Explain that *alliteration* is the repetition of the same consonant sound at the beginning of words. Here are two sentences that use alliteration:

   **G**obs of **g**oopy **g**lop spilled on the **g**round.

   **T**wo **t**all **t**ailors **t**raded **t**op hats for **t**rousers.

2. Students write sentences using alliteration.

▶ **Variations**

- Write alliterations using the names of each person in the class.

   **L**uke **l**istened to **l**oons in **L**ondon.

- Use alliteration with rhyme.

   A **d**og **d**ozed near the **d**oor.

   A **f**inch **f**eather **f**ell on the **f**loor.

The **c**at **c**rept near the **c**ow.

A **b**reeze **b**rushed against the **b**are tree **b**ranches.

A **f**eather **f**ell off the **f**inch.

# Sound Words
### by Kathy Mattenklodt

▶ **Materials:** paper, pencils, crayons, marking pens, or colored pencils (optional)

▶ **Here's How!**

1. Write words such as *creak, gobble, drip, bang,* and *thud* on the chalkboard.

2. Talk about "sound words" with the class. Explain that the use of words that sound like the noise they represent is called *onomatopoeia*.

3. Make a list of sound words as a whole group, in small groups, or independently.

4. Classify the words into categories, such as:

   | animal sounds | weather sounds | thing sounds |
   | people sounds | machinery sounds |

▶ **Variation**

Assign one onomatopoeic word to each student. Students write the word on a piece of drawing paper and illustrate it. Bind the drawings into a class book.

---

**Onomatopoeic Words**

ah-choo  baa  bong  bow-wow  burp  buzz  caw  chirp  choo-choo  clang  clatter  click  clip-clop  cluck  crackle  crinkle  croak  ding-dong  drip  eek  fizz  growl  grunt  hee-haw  hiccup  hiss  hoot  meow  moo  neigh  oink  pitter-patter  plop  purr  quack  rat-a-tat  rattle  rustle  screech  sizzle  smack  snap  snort  splash  squeak  swish  tick-tock  thud  tinkle  toot  twang  varoom  shush  wow  yikes  zip  zoom

---

# It's Not What It Seems

by Kathy Mattenklodt

▶ **Materials:** idiomatic expressions on slips of paper, chart paper, crayons

▶ **Here's How!**

An *idiomatic expression* is one that can't be understood literally. Most conjure up rather humorous mental images.

1. In advance, write idiomatic expressions from the list below on slips of paper. Underline the idioms. Fold the papers in half.

2. Divide students into groups of four. Give each group a piece of chart paper and crayons.

3. Each group picks a slip of paper containing an idiom.

4. Give the groups 3 minutes to draw a simple sketch (stick figures, as well as one-color drawings, are fine) that illustrates the literal meaning of the idiom.

5. Groups share their drawings with the class, who try to name the idiom illustrated.

6. Encourage your students to be idiom gatherers. Keep lists of the idioms found.

**Examples**

he's really <u>on the ball</u>
that <u>drives me up a wall</u>
he <u>paid through the nose</u> for those tickets
she <u>jumped down my throat</u>
I bought it <u>for a song</u>
time to <u>hit the hay</u>
the car <u>hugged the road</u>
the actress <u>stole the spotlight</u>
I <u>heard it through the grapevine</u>
he was <u>on cloud nine</u>
that car is <u>a real lemon</u>

we <u>bent over backward</u> for him
we sat around <u>shooting the breeze</u>
you've got baseball <u>on the brain</u>
the movie was <u>for the birds</u>
the math test was <u>a piece of cake</u>
she <u>turned a cold shoulder</u> to us
don't <u>beat around the bush</u>
that really <u>gets my goat</u>
I'm <u>all ears</u>
just <u>hold your horses</u>

# Longest List
### by Delana Heidrich

▶ **Materials:** chalkboard, chalk, paper, pencils

▶ **Here's How!**

1. Divide your class into three or four teams. Instruct each team to select a recorder.

2. Write the following phrase on the chalkboard: " _____ Words," filling the blank with a single-word category such as one of the examples provided in the box below.

3. Instruct students in each group to call out words that fit in the category. Recorders number and write all group responses. Remind students to call out their words quietly so that other groups do not "steal" their responses.

4. The group with the longest list of category-related words at the end of 1 minute wins the round.

5. The winning group gets to read its list. Other groups may add words not contained on the winning list.

6. Continue play, using a new category for each 1-minute round.

---

**Examples of Categories**

Circus   Camping   School   Kitchen   Farm   Jungle   Sports   Music   Art   Christmas

---

# Wordstorms

by Martha Cheney

▶ **Materials:** chart paper, marker

▶ **Here's How!**

1. Ask students to brainstorm words that fit in one of any number of fun categories.

2. Chart their responses.

3. Post the charts and allow students to add to them whenever they think of a new word that belongs.

**Examples of Categories**
Words that sound beautiful
Words that sound unpleasant
Noisy words
Delicious words
Tactile words
Emotional words

Color Words

magenta
chartreuse
mauve
puce

▶ **Variation**

Post one of the "wordstorm" charts in front of the class. Ask students to do a "quick write" based on a word of their choosing. Students write for 3 to 5 minutes in a stream-of-consciousness manner. Allow time for those students who wish to share their writings. Have students keep their papers in a writing folder so they will have access to their ideas for future writing assignments.

# Whether the Weather

by Jodee Mueller & David Gerk

▶ **Materials:** paper, pencils

▶ **Here's How!**

1. Discuss the day's weather. What words describe it?

2. As a class, generate a list of words to describe weather in general.

3. Choose one of the words and write an acrostic poem about the weather. (Do this together if your class has not written acrostics before.)

   • Write the word in all caps vertically.

   • Add words or phrases horizontally that fit into the vertical word.

### Words That Describe Weather

| warm | sunny | bright | hot | humid | sticky | dry |
|------|-------|--------|-----|-------|--------|-----|
| windy | blustery | blowing | balmy | breezy | nice | |
| rainy | icy | drizzly | drippy | foggy | pleasant | |
| cold | freezing | frigid | frozen | snowy | sleety | |

# Mystery Word
by Kathy Mattenklodt

▶ **Materials:** paper, pencils

▶ **Here's How!**

1. Think of a word.

2. Give clues about the spelling and meaning of the word.

3. Give information until students are able to name the word correctly.

**Examples**

This word begins with the letter *t.*
It ends with a silent *e.*
It contains an *r*-controlled vowel.
It is a noun that names a reptile.
What is the mystery word?
(turtle)

This word begins with a consonant digraph.
Double *t*'s are found in the middle.
It ends with the abbreviation of "emergency room."
It is a verb.
The definition is "to talk fast and foolishly."
What is the mystery word?
(chatter)

This is a five-letter word.
It has a short *a* and a short *i.*
It might describe an airplane, a race car, or a train.
A synonym for the word is *fast.*
What is the mystery word?
(rapid)

# Silly Spelling Stories

by Laurie Williams

▶ **Materials:** weekly spelling list, chalkboard, chalk

▶ **Here's How!**

1. Write the current week's spelling words on the chalkboard. Say the first sentence of a story, incorporating one spelling word.

2. Call on a student to continue the story with one more sentence, using another spelling word.

3. As each spelling word is used, it can be modified to make the tense appropriate or by adding a prefix or a suffix.

4. Check off each word on the board as it is used, or students can keep track of remaining words.

5. The story may get sillier and sillier, but students will enjoy using their spelling words or vocabulary words in context in a new way.

▶ **Variation**

Using the current week's spelling words, instruct the students to create a written story using all of the spelling words. This would be fun done in pairs or small groups.

Spelling List

1. mountain
2. boundary
3. amount
4. announce
5. sprout

# I Don't Believe It!

by Tekla White

▶ **Materials:** none

▶ **Here's How!**

1. Do this activity with the whole class the first time. After that, use smaller groups so that students can participate more frequently.

2. Choose one student to be the judge.

3. The first person starts the story with, "Once upon a time there was _____."

4. Each person adds a sentence to the story.

5. At any time, the judge may say, "I don't believe it!" That is the end of the story.

6. The next person starts a new story.

▶ **Variation**

Work with phrases instead of complete sentences.

1. The story begins with "When I was walking to school today, _____."

    Example: *When I was walking to school today, I saw an elephant.*

2. The next person repeats what was said and adds to the sentence.

    Example: *When I was walking to school today, I saw an elephant wearing sneakers.*

3. The next person adds to the sentence.

    Example: *When I was walking to school today, I saw an elephant wearing sneakers and carrying an umbrella.*

4. The game continues until no one can remember all the items mentioned.

# Super Sequences
by Kathy Mattenklodt

▶ **Materials:** chalkboard, chalk

▶ **Here's How!**

1. Divide the class into groups of three or four students. Groups count off so that each student has a number (1, 2, 3, or 4).

2. List five to ten words in order on the chalkboard. (See examples in the box below.)

3. The first student in each group begins telling a story. That student stops when he or she has used the first word on the list in a sentence of the story.

4. Each student, in order, continues the story, attempting to use the next word in the list.

**Sample Word Lists**

| | | | | |
|---|---|---|---|---|
| spy | cowboy | puppy | blizzard | balloon |
| stumbled | galloped | whined | frigid | escaped |
| mystery | abandoned | ball | wilderness | mountain |
| suspicious | rustlers | master | snowshoes | sheriff |
| couterfeit | hero | reunited | remote | reward |

One day a young spy named Seth stumbled onto an amazing mystery. He first became suspicious

# Fast Talk

by Delana Heidrich

▶ **Materials:** none

▶ **Here's How!**

1. Choose one student to be IT. Whisper a one- or two-word topic into IT's ear.

2. Give IT 30 seconds "think" time, then require IT to talk about his or her topic for 30 seconds. IT does not have to use complete sentences, but all words and phrases must be on the topic.

3. Choose as many students to be IT as time allows.

**Fast-Talk Topics**

| | | | | | |
|---|---|---|---|---|---|
| Cars | Movies | Cartoons | Chocolate | TV | Girls/Boys |
| Rules | School | Books | Sports | Pets | Zoo Animals |

▶ **Variations**

* Allow students to choose their own topics.

* Instead of a broad topic, give students an opinion-based statement to defend or attack.

* Conduct a contest to see who can continue talking about a single subject for the longest period of time.

* As an alternative to younger students' show-and-tell time, allow older students to tell school-appropriate jokes to the class for practice in speaking to a crowd.

# Better and Better

by Martha Cheney

▶ **Materials:** prompts written on slips of paper

▶ **Here's How!**

This activity will help your students gain confidence in their public speaking skills.

1. In advance, prepare slips of paper with the following prompts:

    Dogs are better than cats because…

    Waffles are better than pancakes because…

    Rain is better than sunshine because…

    Summer is better than winter because…

    Books are better than movies because…

    Daisies are better than roses because…

    Peanut butter is better than jelly because…

    A bicycle is better than a skateboard because…

2. Call on a student to draw a slip of paper out of a hat or bag. The student must speak for 1 minute on the topic given.

3. Encourage students to speak with confidence and enthusiasm, even if they do not agree with the statement. Explain that their task is to speak persuasively.

▶ **Variations**

- Allow students to create additional prompts for the activity.

- As students gain skill at speaking, gradually increase the time requirement to 3 minutes.

# Terrific Tongue Twisters

by Kathy Mattenklodt

▶ **Materials:** paper, pencils

▶ **Here's How!**

1. Have students share tongue twisters they know. Add some of your own. (See box below.)

2. Challenge students to think up a sentence or phrase that is hard to say. Most of the words should start with the same sound. For example:

   Mary munched on mushy marshmallows.

   Silly Sammy Seal sent Suzie to Sicily.

3. Students try saying their tongue twisters to a neighbor twice really fast.

4. Students write their tongue twisters on a piece of paper.

5. Collect the tongue twisters and put them in a container where they can be used again and again.

▶ **Variation**

Have students illustrate their tongue twisters and bind them into a "Terrific Tongue Twisters" book.

---

**Examples**
She sells seashells by the seashore.
Peter Piper picked a peck of pickled peppers.
A noisy noise annoys an oyster.
How much wood would a woodchuck chuck if a woodchuck could chuck wood?
rubber baby buggy bumpers rubber baby buggy bumpers rubber baby buggy bumpers
toy boat toy boat toy boat toy boat toy boat toy boat toy boat toy boat toy boat toy boat
Greek grapes Greek grapes Greek grapes Greek grapes Greek grapes Greek grapes

---

# What Did You Say?

by Tekla White

▶ **Materials:** sentences written on individual papers, box or bag, paper, pencils, chalkboard, overhead projector

▶ **Here's How!**

1. In advance, write a different sentence on a piece of paper for each group of students and place them in a box or bag. (See box below.)

2. Divide the students into groups of four to six students.

3. The first group selects a sentence from the box or bag.

4. The group writes the subject nouns on the chalkboard for the class to see.

5. The group acts out the sentence without talking.

6. The groups not performing write what they think the sentence is.

7. The actors write their sentence on the board or overhead projector.

8. The class compares the sentences.

---

**Example Sentences with the Subject Underlined**

<u>Alice and Jeremy</u> waded in the water and had a water fight.
<u>Marvin</u> tied his horse to the fence and brushed and groomed him.
<u>The circus clown</u> beeped his nose like a horn and made sad and funny faces at the children.
<u>Alex</u> put on his tennis shoes and tied them with a double knot.
<u>Mabel</u> looked for her kitten in the garden.
<u>Arnold</u> cut the pie in eight pieces, put each piece on a plate, and set the plates on the table.
<u>Sarah and Ted</u> dug a hole in the garden and planted the little tree.

---

# How-To

by Delana Heidrich

▶ **Materials:** paper, pencils

▶ **Here's How!**

1. Students write instructions for completing any simple classroom activity. The instructions must be written in individually identified steps.

**Examples**

| | |
|---|---|
| getting a book from the bookshelf | turning in a paper |
| drawing a circle | heading a paper |
| tying a shoe | getting a drink of water |
| sharpening a pencil | folding a paper in half |

2. When students have finished writing, invite one student to read the steps aloud as another student follows the steps.

3. Evaluate the writer's instruction-writing skill. Could the student follow the steps without further explanation? Were any steps left out? Could the student complete the task?

▶ **Variations**

• Students write the steps for learning a skill (riding a bicycle), making a favorite snack (cheese and crackers), or completing some other task. See if classmates can guess the task.

• Students write the rules of a popular sport. Compare and contrast student writings. Did students include the same rules? Were the same rules stated in different ways?

# Movements and Mannerisms

by Delana Heidrich

▶ **Materials:** paper, pencils

▶ **Here's How!**

1. Students write a single-paragraph description of one other student in the class.

### What You Can and Cannot Say

**Not Okay**

1. Current physical descriptions:
   *This person is wearing a dress.*

2. Comments that relate person to you:
   *This person is on my baseball team.*

3. Put-downs:
   *This person never turns in his work.*

4. Negative personality traits:
   *This person is a bully.*

**Okay**

1. General physical descriptions:
   *This person frequently wears a dress.*

2. Comments that relate person to a group:
   *This person plays on a baseball team.*

3. Funny, harmless remarks:
   *This person leans back in his chair a lot and sometimes falls over.*

4. Positive personality traits:
   *This person is humorous.*

2. At the bottom of the paragraph, direct each student to write the name of the person described.

3. Students fold their papers in half and hand them in.

4. Use another 10-minute period to read the descriptions. (This will allow you to edit out statements that do not follow the guidelines.) Allow students to guess the identities of classmates.

# Get 'Em Hooked

by Delana Heidrich

▶ **Materials:** overhead projector, paper, pencils

▶ **Here's How!**

1. In advance, write the topic and sentence at right on an overhead transparency.

2. Tell students that a good story always starts with a sentence that grabs the reader's attention. Share the sample written on the transparency.

3. Write another topic on the overhead. (Choose from the suggestions in the box below or create a topic of your own.)

Topic: A Thrilling Ride

As the car started to accelerate down the steep hill, Harry realized that the brakes were gone!

4. Challenge students to write an attention-grabbing first line.

5. Allow students to read their first lines. Discuss what words, phrases, or ideas in this line helped "hook" the reader. Point out that topics can be addressed in a multitude of equally effective ways. Explain that finding your own way to start writing about a topic is how you develop an individual style.

**Suggested Topics**

| | | | |
|---|---|---|---|
| a beloved pet | my favorite holiday | relatives | weather |
| zoo animals | country living | baseball | school |
| best friends | yuk! | time travel | wishful thinking |

# Phenomenal Partner Paragraphs
### by Kathy Mattenklodt

▶ **Materials:** chalkboard or overhead projector, paper, pencils

▶ **Here's How!**

1. Divide students into groups of four and assign each student in each group a number, 1 through 4.

2. Give each group a piece of lined paper and a pencil.

3. Pick a topic from the list below or choose a topic from class studies and write it for the groups to see.

4. Student 1 writes a topic sentence on the paper.

5. Student 1 then passes the paper to Student 2.

6. Student 2 reads the topic sentence and adds a supporting detail.

7. Students 3 and 4 each add a supporting detail.

8. Groups read their paragraphs and revise as needed before sharing with the class.

**Sample Topics**

bananas   autumn (or any season)   worms   balloons   exercise   snow   kites
spaghetti   clouds   spelling tests   recess   shoes   happiness   the sun

▶ **Variation**

Require that the paragraphs be in a specific style of writing—persuasive, narrative, descriptive, etc.

# Prove It!

by Delana Heidrich

▶ **Materials:** chalkboard or overhead projector, paper, pencils

▶ **Here's How!**

1. Write one of the sample sentences from the box below on the chalkboard or overhead projector.

2. Tell students that they must "prove" this sentence through descriptive writing. They may not "tell" the reader the content of the sentence. For example:

   To prove the sentence "The room was a mess," you may *not* write "The room was a disaster." Instead, you could write "Candy wrappers cluttered the floor, puddles of pop flooded the countertops, and puzzle pieces covered the couch."

3. Allow 5 minutes for students to write.

4. Share writing in small groups or as a class.

---

**Sentences to Prove**

Mom was incredibly busy!
Babies are so cute!
My dog loves me.
I was terrified!

Cafeteria food is disgusting!
The house was spotless.
I stumbled around in complete darkness.
She was the finest athlete in the school.

---

▶ **Variations**

- Instruct students to write a clear description of a common household item such as a pencil, without ever naming the item they are describing.

- Have students create their own sentences to "prove" through description.

# Secret Pals

by Kathy Mattenklodt

▶ **Materials:** students' names on slips of paper, container, paper, pencils

▶ **Here's How!**

1. In advance, write out the students' names on slips of paper.

2. Have each student in the class draw another student's name out of a bag, hat, etc.

3. Instruct the students to write a special message to their "Secret Pals," telling them something that will make them feel special and important. (See the example below.)

4. Students fold their messages and write the "Pal's" name on the outside.

5. Distribute the messages during a recess or before school the next day.

6. Try to allow several more time slots during the week to write more special notes. The Secret Pals should reveal their identities in the last note.

Will,

Thanks for helping me with my homework this week. I enjoyed visiting with you at lunchtime.

Your Secret Pal

# Word Pyramid

by Kathy Mattenklodt

▶ **Materials:** paper, pencils

▶ **Here's How!**

Do this activity several times as a class before expecting students to do it independently.

1. Line 1: Choose a one-word topic.

2. Line 2: Write two words describing the topic.

3. Line 3: Write three words that show action of the topic.

4. Line 4: Write four words describing a feeling about the topic.

5. Line 5: Write five words explaining knowledge of the topic.

| Sports | Books |
|---|---|
| exciting, fun | word pictures |
| crowning new champions | take you places |
| hoping to be victorious | they are good friends |
| recreation, competition, and physical activity | adventure, mystery, fantasy, science fiction |

▶ **Variations**

- Have pairs of students write a Word Pyramid about a character from literature or from history and share it with the class.

- Have students write a Word Pyramid describing individual classmates.

# Essay Question Survival Skills
by Delana Heidrich

▶ **Materials:** chart paper or overhead transparency, paper and pencils (optional)

▶ **Here's How!**

1. In advance, prepare a chart or overhead transparency listing the verbs at right that are commonly used in expository writing prompts.

2. Read the list to students. Explain that the words are often used in directions for essays and that it is important to understand their meanings.

3. Pick one of the words and discuss its meaning.

4. Then use one of the verbs to create a question that requires no research or specialized knowledge to answer. (See suggested questions below.)

5. Ask students for either verbal or written responses to your question.

6. In subsequent lessons, ask questions for each of the verbs listed.

Compare
Contrast
Define
List
Give your opinion
Explain
Justify
Highlight
Summarize
State

**Expository Writing Verbs**

**Compare** (candy to cookies, apples to oranges, your home to a friend's home)
**Contrast** (day and night, dogs and cats, tennis shoes and sandals)
**Define** (classroom, a tree, the game of baseball)
**List** (subjects you study, items on a fast-food menu, animals in a zoo)
**Give your opinion** (of the food in the cafeteria, of television shows, of math tests)
**Explain** (how to throw a ball, how we head our papers, how to check out a library book)
**Justify** (why you should get a larger allowance, why you should be allowed to stay up later)
**Highlight** (the events of this school year, your last birthday, a vacation trip)
**Summarize** (the last fiction book you read, a favorite movie, what you know about _____ )
**State** (a problem the school faces, the classroom rules, your name and address)

# Alphabet Twins

### by Tekla White

▶ **Materials:** large chart paper and markers, dictionaries

▶ **Here's How!**

1. Divide the class into groups of four.

2. Each group writes the names of their group members at the top of the paper.

3. Groups have 5 minutes to write as many words as they can that have double letters. The words need to be written large enough to be viewed when posted.

4. When time is called, groups compute their scores.

Team 1
soon
vacuum
fill
button

**Scoring**
- a double vowel is 2 points (soon, vacuum)
- a double consonant is 1 point (fill, button)
- a word with more than one set of double letters scores triple points

For example: *balloon* scores 2 points for *oo*, 1 point for *ll*; that's 3 points, tripled = 9 points

5. Groups post their papers on a board or wall with their scores.

6. Students survey the posted words.

7. Groups challenge any words they find that are misspelled by looking up the word in the dictionary and writing the correct spelling.

8. If a word is misspelled, the group that posted the word must subtract the points they received for the word. The group that found the error receives 3 points.

▶ **Variation**

Choose two teams. Team 1 writes words with double letters on the board or overhead projector. Team 2 checks the spelling in the dictionary.

# Letter Ghosts
### by Tekla White

▶ **Materials:** chalkboard or overhead projector, paper, pencils

▶ **Here's How!**

1. Divide the class into two teams.

2. Teams brainstorm and record as many "ghostly" words as they can that have silent letters.

3. Team 1 writes a word on the board or overhead projector.

4. Team 2 writes the next word.

5. The teams take turns writing the words until a team runs out of ghostly words.

6. The group that writes the last word is the winner.

---

**Game Rules**

Ghostly letters are seen and never heard.
The *h* in *ghost* is a good example.

Blends like *ch* don't count.
Words can't be repeated.

---

▶ **Variation**

Each student writes a ghostly word on white paper. The silent letters are written with white crayon and then outlined with black; the other letters are written in different colors. The words may be decorated or illustrated. Display the results.

# Word Pursuit

by Kathy Mattenklodt

▶ **Materials:** paper, pencils

▶ **Here's How!**

1. Choose an interesting vocabulary word that students are not familiar with—the bigger the better. Briefly explain the word's meaning.

2. Have students find as many words as they can within the big word. Sort the words by three-, four-, five-, and six-letter words.

3. Share students' lists with the class.

catastrophic
cat
strip
stop
cast
hop

**Word Ideas**

| | | |
|---|---|---|
| catastrophic | exponential | mortification |
| chronological | imperceptible | pandemonium |
| contemporary | insurmountable | prognostication |
| contemptuous | intermittent | tonsillectomy |
| empathetic | investigation | voluminous |

# Spell Right

by Tekla White

▶ **Materials:** spelling words on slips of paper, paper bag for each group

▶ **Here's How!**

1. In advance, write one spelling word on each slip of paper and put them in bags, one bag for each group.

2. Divide the class into groups of eight or fewer. Each group gathers in a separate area of the room and sits in a circle.

3. Students in each group number off to determine the order of their turns.

4. Each group plays among themselves, following these rules:

   • The first student draws a spelling word from the bag and says the word.

   • The next person spells it.

   • The person holding the word checks the spelling.

   If the spelling is correct, the speller draws another word from the bag and asks the next person to spell it.

   If the spelling is incorrect, the person who drew the word spells it correctly for the group and draws a new word for the next speller.

   • The words always go back in the bag after they are spelled.

   The word may be drawn more than once, so students have to pay attention when a word is spelled.

Spell mountain.

m-o-u-n-t-a-i-n

# Alphabet Squares

by Delana Heidrich

▶ **Materials:** chalkboard, paper, pencils

▶ **Here's How!**

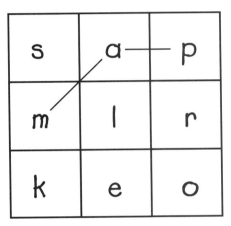

1. Draw a nine-square grid (like a tic-tac-toe board) on the chalkboard.

2. Write a letter in each square of the grid, being certain to include at least two vowels.

3. Challenge students to make and list words of three or more letters by connecting letters in the grid. The rules are:

   • You may connect letters up, down, or across.

   • The letters can be used again for a new word.

   • A letter can be used only once in each word.

4. Show the example given above.

5. At the end of a specified time, see who has the longest list of words.

▶ **Variations**

   • Divide the class into teams, rather than requiring individual play.

   • Challenge students to connect as many words as possible in the style of a crossword puzzle, using graph paper.

# Lists, Lists, and More Lists

by Kathy Mattenklodt

▶ **Materials:** paper, pencils

▶ **Here's How!**

These challenges are more interesting when posed to cooperative groups. Do one challenge at a time. Be sure to compile lists and post so that students may use them in written work.

**1.** Have students create lists using the following suffixes:

Words that end in *-tion*
Words that end in *-able*
Words that end in *-ly*
Words that end in *-ful*
Words that end in *-ment*

**2.** Have students create lists using the following prefixes:

Words that begin with *un*
Words that begin with *re*
Words that begin with *dis*
Words that begin with *mis*
Words that begin with *auto*

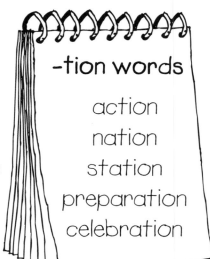

-tion words

action
nation
station
preparation
celebration

# Triangle Words
by Martha Cheney

▶ **Materials:** chalkboard or overhead projector

▶ **Here's How!**

1. Write a vowel on the chalkboard or overhead.

2. Ask students to think of a letter that could be added to the vowel to create a two-letter word.

3. Next, ask for a letter that can be added to create a three-letter word. (It is okay to rearrange the order of the letters.)

4. Write each word beneath the previous word to create a triangle shape.

5. Continue adding a letter at a time until the group can no longer form a new word.

# Color-Coded Sentences

by Laurie Williams

▶ **Materials:** chalkboard or overhead projector, paper and pencils (optional)

▶ **Here's How!**

1. On the chalkboard or overhead projector, write the words shown at right.

2. Then write a series of colors in the order a sentence might be constructed. For example:

| red | green | yellow |
|-----|-------|--------|
| (adjective) | (noun) | (verb) |

3. Students must come up with sentences that fit the color pattern. This may be done orally or in writing by individuals, pairs, or small groups.

| noun: | green |
|-------|-------|
| verb: | yellow |
| adjective: | red |
| adverb: | blue |

**Examples of Patterns and Sentences**

1. red    red    green    yellow    red    green
   *Small brown squirrels collect many nuts.*

2. red    red    green    yellow    green    blue
   *Some beginning singers get laryngitis often.*

▶ **Variations**

• Have students make up their own color patterns for other students to solve.

• Have students match sentences to the color patterns they represent.

# In a Word

by Jodee Mueller & David Gerk

▶ **Materials:** newspaper or magazine, paper, pencils

▶ **Here's How!**

1. Post a large picture from a newspaper or magazine where everyone can see it.

2. Have students write down five nouns, five verbs, and five adjectives to describe what they see in the picture. If, for example, the picture showed a football game, the words might be similar to the following:

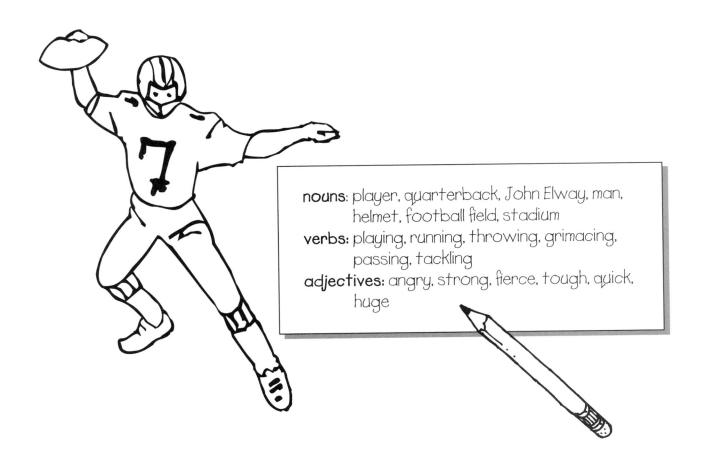

**nouns:** player, quarterback, John Elway, man, helmet, football field, stadium

**verbs:** playing, running, throwing, grimacing, passing, tackling

**adjectives:** angry, strong, fierce, tough, quick, huge

# Common or Proper?

by Jodee Mueller & David Gerk

▶ **Materials:** paper, pencils

▶ **Here's How!**

1. Students fold a sheet of paper in half lengthwise.

2. Label the left-hand column "Proper Nouns" and the right-hand column "Common Nouns."

3. Give students a prescribed amount of time to look around the room and list all the proper nouns and common nouns they see.

   • They may NOT use classmates' names.

   • Hint: Brand names are proper nouns.

4. Have students share a unique noun from their lists.

5. Form groups of four to combine individual lists into a group list. Which group has the most entries?

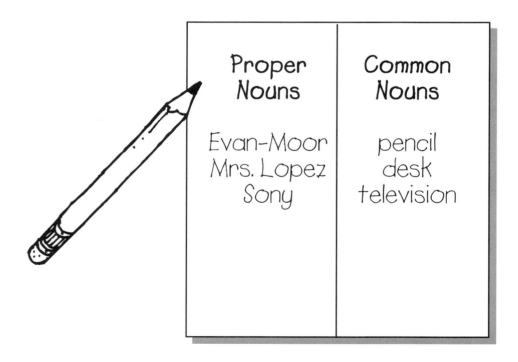

| Proper Nouns | Common Nouns |
|---|---|
| Evan-Moor | pencil |
| Mrs. Lopez | desk |
| Sony | television |

# Tell Me More

by Tekla White

▶ **Materials:** none

▶ **Here's How!**

1. Divide students into groups of three. Walk around the room listening to the groups.

2. Within each group,

   - the first person says a noun

   - the next person adds *the* and an adjective describing the noun

   - the third person finishes the sentence and gives another noun

3. Encourage students to use different adjectives and nouns each time they start a new assembly-line sentence. The game continues until you call time.

▶ **Variation**

1. The first person writes a noun on a piece of paper or an individual dry-erase board.

2. The second person writes a sentence using that noun and an adjective.

3. The third person underlines the noun and circles the adjective.

# Word Teams

## by Tekla White

▶ **Materials:** none

▶ **Here's How!**

1. Divide the class into teams of four. Determine the order in which teams will participate.

2. The first team states a noun and action verb. The whole team must agree upon this, or teams may decide to allow members to take turns providing the core sentence. For example:

   Elsie ran.

3. The next team repeats the noun and verb and then adds an adverb that ends in *ly*. For example:

   Elsie ran quickly.

4. If a team can't add a word ending in *ly,* the next team has a turn. If a team does add any *ly* word, they get a point.

5. The next team then provides a core sentence.

6. The team that names the most adverbs ending in *ly* is the winner.

# May They Rest in Peace

by Delana Heidrich

▶ **Materials:** large tombstones on chart paper, black marking pen

▶ **Here's How!**

1. In advance, draw a large tombstone on several pieces of chart paper and write "R.I.P." on each.

2. Ask students if anyone can explain what "R.I.P" means. If no one offers a meaning, explain that it means "rest in peace." Then say, "We are going to lay to rest some very overused, boring words that keep writing from being interesting."

3. Write an overused adjective or adverb on the tombstone. (See box below.)

4. Challenge students to come up with a list of words to use in place of the overused word.

5. When students run out of alternative adjectives or adverbs for your first word, add any they may have overlooked.

6. Write another overused adjective or adverb on a new chart and begin a new list.

---

**Overused Adjectives and Adverbs**

Nice:  kind, polite, fine, pleasant, enjoyable, agreeable, pleasing, lovely, satisfying, charming, exquisite

Good:  fine, outstanding, superior, excellent, first-rate, first-class, exceptional, terrific, stupendous, marvelous, dazzling

Fun:  amusing, hilarious, entertaining, invigorating, enjoyable, pleasurable, stimulating, energizing, revitalizing

Really:  actually, truly, certainly (see *Very*)

---

# Silent Name Game
by Laurie Williams

▶ **Materials:** none

▶ **Here's How!**

1. Without talking or making any sounds, students line themselves up across the classroom in alphabetical order by first names only.

2. After all students have lined up, call out names of students (one at a time) not in the classroom and have students who would be DIRECTLY in front of and DIRECTLY behind that student alphabetically raise their hands.

▶ **Variation**

Line up by last names or middle names. If students don't know each other's last or middle names, they should think of a nonverbal sign for letting others know the spelling, such as sign language or making their fingers look like the letters.

# Dictionary Wars

by Delana Heidrich

▶ **Materials:** dictionaries, chalkboard, chalk

▶ **Here's How!**

1. Divide the class into groups of four students. Each student needs a dictionary. (Note: By playing in groups, the entire class does not need the same edition.)

2. Write a word on the chalkboard.

3. Each student must find the word in the dictionary and place a finger on it. When all members of a group have located the word, they raise their hands.

4. Award 4 points to the first group with all hands raised, 3 to the next group, 2 to the third group, and 1 point to each remaining group. (Be sure to verify that all members of a group have located the word before points are official.)

# Guide Word Giggles

by Laurie Williams

▶ **Materials:** index cards with vocabulary words

▶ **Here's How!**

1. In advance of the activity, prepare several sets of eight index cards, each card containing one unique vocabulary word. Hint: Use the glossary of a textbook and choose words that are near each other alphabetically.

2. After a lesson on guide words, hand out one set of index cards to eight students. Each student will "be" the vocabulary word on their card.

3. Choose two students to be the "guide words." Those two students stand in front of the class and hold up their index cards for the other students to see.

4. One at a time, seated students with vocabulary word cards come to the front of the room and position themselves alphabetically in relation to the guide words and to all the other students who have preceded them.

5. Seated students without cards confirm the correctness of each standing student's position.

6. Pass out another set of index cards, choose two more guide words, and play again.

▶ **Variation**

Have students silently line up across the front of the room from left to right alphabetically according to the word on their card.

# Dictionary Duos

by Tekla White

▶ **Materials:** dictionaries, paper, pencils, chalkboard or overhead projector

▶ **Here's How!**

1. Write a numbered list of five spelling or reading words on the chalkboard or overhead projector.

2. Students work in pairs to find the words in the dictionary and then write the guide words used on the page where the word is listed.

3. Students volunteer the answers, which may be checked by the class.

4. If a pair has five correct answers, their names may be displayed on a Dictionary Champions list on the board.

# Scavenger Hunt
by Kathy Mattenklodt

▶ **Materials:** chalkboard, chalk, paper, pencils, books

▶ **Here's How!**

1. Write the list at right on the chalkboard.

2. Divide students into pairs. Give each pair paper and a pencil. Number the paper to five.

3. Tell students they are going on a scavenger hunt! They must locate all the items on the list and write down each item. They must find each item in a different book.

> 1. textbook title
> 2. fiction book title
> 3. an author
> 4. an illustrator
> 5. a publication date
> 6. a publisher

4. Allow 5 minutes for students to search. (It will be noisy!) You might want to set simple ground rules, such as:

   • You must walk.

   • You may not grab an item from another pair.

   • Use conversational voices.

5. Have students share their findings.

# Hink Pink

### Old Favorite

▶ **Materials:** none

▶ **Here's How!**

1. Define *hink pink* for students. *Hink pink* means a pair of one-syllable rhyming words that answer a clue.

   A hink pink for *overweight feline* is *fat cat*.
   A hink pink for *happy father* is *glad dad*.
   A hink pink for *naughty boy* is *bad lad*.

2. Choose hink pinks and then hinky pinkies (two syllables) from the list below to challenge your students. As you play this game more times, you may move on to *hinkity pinkity* (three syllables) and even *hinkinkity pinkinkity* (four syllables). Encourage your students to bring clues from home and build a class list.

**Hink Pink**

| | | | |
|---|---|---|---|
| azure footwear | blue shoe | beige vehicle | tan van |
| cold pond | cool pool | evening illumination | night light |
| unique grizzly | rare bear | solid nightcrawler | firm worm |
| Smokey's seat | bear chair | pie wagon | tart cart |
| impolite man | rude dude | high fence | tall wall |
| tiny sphere | small ball | chicken cage | hen pen |
| twisted penny | bent cent | cattle food | cow chow |
| noisy group | loud crowd | poultry movie | chick flick |

**Hinky Pinky**

| | | | |
|---|---|---|---|
| hilarious rabbit | funny bunny | amusing cat | witty kitty |
| kingly dog | regal beagle | drenched canine | soggy doggy |
| inactive flower | lazy daisy | fuzzy fruit | hairy berry |
| posy strength | flower power | chanticleer fan | rooster booster |

# Awesome Analogies

by Kathy Mattenklodt

▶ **Materials:** chalkboard and chalk

▶ **Here's How!**

1. Analogies can be a great thinking activity to fill a few minutes. Teach the symbols used in analogies:

   - up **is to** down **as** in **is to** out

   - up : down :: in : out

2. Write an analogy on the chalkboard. Leave out any one or two of the four parts. Use the list below to get you started.

3. Students respond with the missing words.

### Analogy Examples

healthy : healthier :: healthier : healthiest
owl : bird :: (any animal) : (its classification)
half : hemi :: one : uni
fiction : fact :: love : hate
divide : separate :: flat : level
breakfast : lunch :: afternoon : evening
cold : freeze :: hot : melt
three: six :: four : eight
intelligent : brilliant :: hungry : starving
she : he :: her : him
eat : ate :: sleep : slept
room : house :: branch : tree

hand : write :: bell : ring
peach : fruit :: fork : silverware
computer : office (school) :: tractor : farm
book : read :: food : eat
pool : swimmer :: microscope : scientist
moon : earth :: earth : sun
book : character :: recipe : ingredient
chicken : rooster :: horse : stallion
athlete : team :: state (province) : country
crib : baby :: guitar : musician
wrist : hand :: ankle : foot

# Alphabet Sentences

by Delana Heidrich

▶ **Materials:** scratch paper, pencils

▶ **Here's How!**

1. Divide students into small groups.

2. Challenge each group to create a four-word sentence using words that begin with ABCD, in that order. The sentences may be silly, but they must be grammatically correct. For example:

    Ants buy chocolate doughnuts.

    Aunt Betty collects dolls.

    Always bite carrots delicately.

    A big caterpillar drooled.

3. Allow time to share sentences.

4. Next, challenge groups to build five-word sentences (ABCDE).

▶ **Variation**

Have students create sentences in which all words have the same number of syllables.

# Nicknames

by Delana Heidrich

▶ **Materials:** none

▶ **Here's How!**

1. Explain that a nickname is a descriptive name given to a person in addition to or instead of his or her given name. For example, a really tall person might be nicknamed "Stretch" or "Stilt." A person who likes to sing might be nicknamed "Rock Star" or "The Voice."

2. Tell students they are going to choose a nickname for themselves and tell why they chose that name. For example:

   *If I could choose a nickname for myself, it would be "Cowgirl" because I like to ride horses.*

   Remind students that the nickname they choose should say something about their personality, appearance, mannerisms, behaviors, or hobbies.

3. Give students 30 seconds or so to think before sharing their nicknames with a partner.

4. Have students share their nicknames with the class.

▶ **Variations**

- Have students choose uplifting nicknames for classmates.

- Have students choose nicknames for classmates without naming the classmate. Then challenge other students to guess who is being named. For example:

   *If I could choose a nickname for someone in this class, it would be "Book Worm" because she loves to read. Guess who I have named.*

# Puzzling Palindromes

by Kathy Mattenklodt

▶ **Materials:** paper, pencils

▶ **Here's How!**

1. Divide students into groups of four.

2. Explain to students that *palindromes* are words that are spelled the same forward and backward, for example, *noon* or *mom*.

3. Challenge groups to think of as many palindromes as they can and write them on a piece of paper.

4. Combine lists from all groups onto a class chart. Your students are likely to add to the list over time.

**Examples of Palindromes**

| | | | | | | | | | | | |
|------|------|------|------|-------|-------|------|-------|-------|-------|-------|------|
| dad | pop | eye | gag | eve | bob | did | dud | tot | nun | SOS | deed |
| Otto | peep | sees | toot | radar | civic | refer | rotor | kayak | level | madam | |

▶ **Variation**

Share these sentence and phrase palindromes with your students.

A man, a plan, a canal, Panama!

Madam, I'm Adam.

Never odd or even.

Step on no pets.

Was it a car or a cat I saw?

# "Sum"-thing Spectacular

by Kathy Mattenklodt

▶ **Materials:** chart paper, paper, pencils

▶ **Here's How!**

1. Prepare a chart that assigns each letter of the alphabet a numerical value.

2. Have students create words whose letters would equal a given sum.

3. Let pairs of students check each other's words.

4. Share results as time permits.

| | | |
|---|---|---|
| A = 1 | J = 10 | S = 19 |
| B = 2 | K = 11 | T = 20 |
| C = 3 | L = 12 | U = 21 |
| D = 4 | M = 13 | V = 22 |
| E = 5 | N = 14 | W = 23 |
| F = 6 | O = 15 | X = 24 |
| G = 7 | P = 16 | Y = 25 |
| H = 8 | Q = 17 | Z = 26 |
| I = 9 | R = 18 | |

**Try these:**

Three-letter word with the sum of 18
Four-letter word with the sum of 18
Five-letter word with the sum of 24
Six-letter word with the sum of 32
Any word with the sum of 50
Any word with the sum of 100

# Who's on Deck?

by Ethel Condon

▶ **Materials:** deck of cards for each pair of students

▶ **Here's How!**

1. Divide students into partners and give each pair a deck of cards.

2. Students remove the face cards from the deck, deal the remaining cards, and place their stacks of cards face down.

3. Tell students which computation operation they will be practicing—addition, subtraction, or multiplication.

4. Each student turns over the top card of his or her deck.

5. Students perform the designated operation using those two numbers.

6. The first one with the correct answer gets to keep the two cards.

7. When the two stacks have been used or time is called, students count their cards to see who has the most cards.

addition

# Catch!

by Ethel Condon

▶ **Materials:** rubber ball or Nerf® ball, permanent marker

▶ **Here's How!**

1. In advance, using a permanent marker, write basic number fact problems all over the surface of the ball. Use all four operations.

2. Toss the ball to a student.

3. The student locates the fact closest to his or her right thumb, reads the fact, and gives the answer.

4. The student can either toss the ball back or to another student.

5. Once a class is proficient with their facts, time them to see how many correct answers can be given in 1 minute.

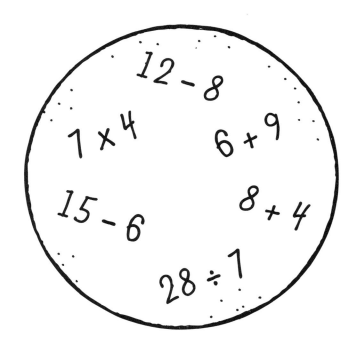

# Multiplication Magic

### by Tekla White

▶ **Materials:** chalkboard and chalk

▶ **Here's How!**

1. Ask students to help you write out the 9s multiplication tables from 9 x 1 to 9 x 9 on the chalkboard.

2. Challenge students to see if they can discover any patterns that make multiplication by 9 easier.

3. After some thinking time, share ideas. Students are likely to observe that the numerals in the ones place begin at 9 and decrease by one. The numerals in the tens place begin at 0 and increase by one.

4. Clarify and summarize student findings by sharing the following information:

   The number in the tens place of the answer is always one less than the number by which 9 is being multiplied. The sum of the two numerals in the answer is always 9. For example:

   9 x 4 = 36 (3 is one less than 4; 3 + 6 = 9)

5. Have students verify that this "magic" works for all the 9s facts.

# We're on a Roll

by Laurie Williams

▶ **Materials:** chalkboard and chalk, dice, paper, pencils

▶ **Here's How!**

1. Divide the class into pairs.

2. Give each pair two dice.

3. Write on the chalkboard the operations you want each group to perform.

4. Each pair rolls their dice. They all mentally add the numbers showing together, then perform each operation listed on the chalkboard. For example:

> Roll the dice. One shows a 6, the other a 4. Add 6 and 4 together to get 10. Then 10 is multiplied by 1, 3, 5, 7, and 9.

# More Nifty Nines

by Tekla White

▶ **Materials:** paper, pencils, calculator for checking answers (optional)

▶ **Here's How!**

1. Divide students into groups of four.

2. Give the groups several two-digit and three-digit numbers to multiply by 9.

3. The groups look for patterns in the answers.

4. Present the following information if no one discovers it:

   The digits in each answer add up to 9 or a multiple of 9.

5. Have the groups test the information. Did they find exceptions to the rule?

6. Discuss how this information can help in judging the reasonableness of an answer.

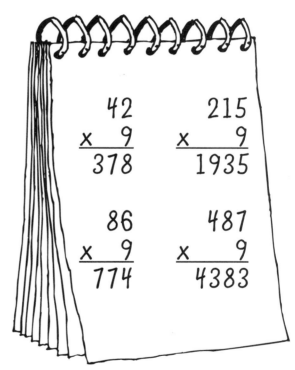

$$\begin{array}{r} 42 \\ \times\ 9 \\ \hline 378 \end{array} \qquad \begin{array}{r} 215 \\ \times\ 9 \\ \hline 1935 \end{array}$$

$$\begin{array}{r} 86 \\ \times\ 9 \\ \hline 774 \end{array} \qquad \begin{array}{r} 487 \\ \times\ 9 \\ \hline 4383 \end{array}$$

# Real-Number Relay

by Delana Heidrich

▶ **Materials:** math textbook, chalkboard, chalk

▶ **Here's How!**

1. Divide the class into evenly-numbered teams.

2. Call out a math problem from your math textbook. Instruct the first member of each team to race (walk quickly) to the chalkboard, write the problem, and then solve it. (Start with a problem that will be easy for students to remember—26 + 47, 15 x 9, etc.)

3. While students are working, write the next problem on the board for each team.

4. As soon as a student completes the problem and returns to his or her seat, the second person on the team goes to the board to answer the new problem.

5. Continue in this manner until each team member has solved a problem.

6. Teams may take time to check their responses and make corrections. When a team thinks all its answers are correct, team members raise their hands.

7. As a group, check all answers. The winner is the first team to raise their hands **and** have all answers correct.

▶ **Variations**

- To cause less commotion, require one team at a time to complete the relay. Time each team with a stopwatch. The winning team is the one that completes the relay in the least amount of time.

- Assign teams a set number of problems in student math textbooks to complete instead of writing problems on the board. Ask teammates to work together to find the answers. The first team to complete the problems with no errors wins.

# Palindrome Play

by Delana Heidrich

▶ **Materials:** chalkboard and chalk, paper, pencils

▶ **Here's How!**

1. Explain to students that a *palindrome* is a number that reads the same, digit for digit, backward and forward. For example, 34,243.

2. Show students how any number can be turned into a palindrome by adding it to its reverse.

$$\begin{array}{r} 532 \\ + 235 \\ \hline 767 \end{array}$$

Some numbers will require more than one step to be transformed into a palindrome. Just keep adding the reverse to the sum until you end up with the palindrome.

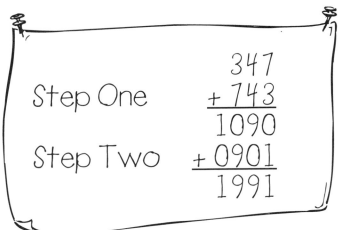

Step One
$$\begin{array}{r} 347 \\ + 743 \\ \hline 1090 \end{array}$$
Step Two
$$\begin{array}{r} + 0901 \\ \hline 1991 \end{array}$$

3. Write a number on the chalkboard for students to turn into a palindrome. Start with one-step palindromes and move on when students are ready.

**Examples of Palindromes**

One-step palindromes: 54, 112, 13, 27, 81, 425, 216
Two-step palindromes: 76, 84, 139, 172, 93, 368, 107
Three-step palindromes: 687, 538, 348, 1687
More-than-three-step palindromes: 29,832 (6), 2158 (6)

▶ **Variation**

Challenge students to come up with numbers that require several steps to reach palindrome status.

# Ladder Math
## by Tekla White

▶ **Materials:** chalkboard, chalk, paper, pencils, calculator to check work (optional)

▶ **Here's How!**

1. On the chalkboard, draw a simple ladder with five rungs.

2. Each student draws the ladder on paper, writes a single-digit number on each of the rungs, adds the single-digit numbers together, and then records the answer on a separate piece of paper.

3. Students exchange ladders with a neighbor. Each must mentally add the numbers on the other's ladder.

4. Share answers. If the written answer is not the same as the mental math, the students may use calculators to check the results.

▶ **Variations**

- Students draw more rungs on the ladder and use more numbers.

- Students use two-digit numbers.

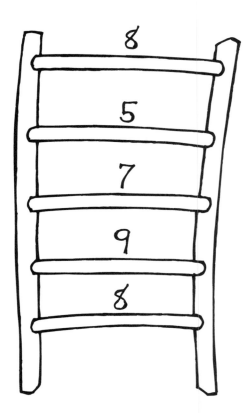

# And the Number Is...
### by Jodee Mueller & David Gerk

▶ **Materials:** paper, pencils, calculators (optional)

▶ **Here's How!**

1. Ask students to follow these steps:

   • Think of a number and write it down.

   • Multiply your number by 2.

   • Add 18 to the product.

   • Divide by 2.

   • Write down your answer.

2. Repeat the steps two more times, starting with a different number each time.

3. What is the pattern? (The ending number is 9 more than the beginning number.)

I see a pattern!

# Sum It Up
by Jodee Mueller & David Gerk

▶ **Materials:** none

▶ **Here's How!**

Make mental math more interesting and challenging with these problems.

1. Start with the number of letters in the alphabet (26)

    add the sides of a pentagon (5)

    add the number of horns on a unicorn (1)

    add the number of wings on a bird (2)

    add the number of legs on a chair (4)

$$\begin{array}{r} 26 \\ 5 \\ 1 \\ 2 \\ +\ 4 \\ \hline 38 \end{array}$$

2. Start with the number of fingers on one hand (5)

    add the number of dimes in a dollar (10)

    add the number of legs on a dog (4)

    add the number of months in a year (12)

    add the number of wheels on a tricycle (3)

$$\begin{array}{r} 5 \\ 10 \\ 4 \\ 12 \\ +\ 3 \\ \hline 34 \end{array}$$

3. Start with the number of sides of a square (4)

    add the number of seconds in a minute (60)

    add the number of legs of a spider (8)

    add the number of quarts in a gallon (4)

    add the number of days in a week (7)

$$\begin{array}{r} 4 \\ 60 \\ 8 \\ 4 \\ +\ 7 \\ \hline 83 \end{array}$$

# Sum Fun

by Martha Cheney

▶ **Materials:** overhead projector and marking pen, or chalkboard and chalk

▶ **Here's How!**

1. On the overhead or chalkboard, draw a large 3 x 3 grid.

2. Write a one-digit number in each box.

3. Challenge students to find which row of numbers (adding across, down, and diagonally) yields the greatest sum and the lowest sum without using pencil and paper.

|   |   |   |
|---|---|---|
| 5 | 3 | 8 |
| 9 | 7 | 2 |
| 1 | 6 | 4 |

▶ **Variation**

Increase the challenge by using two-digit numbers in the grid.

# Days of Our Lives

### by Martha Cheney

▶ **Materials:** chalkboard and chalk, paper, pencils, calculators

▶ **Here's How!**

Challenge students to find out how many days they have been alive. Write a list of leap years on the chalkboard and remind students to take into account any leap years during their lifetimes! (See box below.)

Here are some fun follow-ups:

* In advance, figure the number of days you have been alive. After students have done their own calculations, ask them to estimate the number of days for you.

* What is the difference in days between the ages of the oldest student and the youngest student?

* Ask students to express their ages as mixed numbers, expressing the portion of the year since their last birthday as a fraction of a year.

| **Leap Years Starting with 1940** | | | | | | | | |
|------|------|------|------|------|------|------|------|-----------|
| 1940 | 1944 | 1948 | 1952 | 1956 | 1960 | 1964 | 1968 | 1972 |
| 1976 | 1980 | 1984 | 1988 | 1992 | 1996 | 2000 | 2004 | 2008, etc. |

▶ **Variation**

Calculate the number of hours or minutes students have been alive.

# Don't Forget the Dot

by Tekla White

▶ **Materials:** chalkboard and chalk, or overhead projector and marking pen, paper, pencils

▶ **Here's How!**

1. Write the following problems on the overhead or chalkboard. Write the answer for one problem in each set.

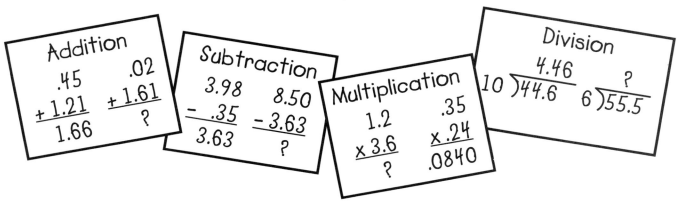

2. Direct students to solve the other problem in each set using the first one as a model. Tell them to think about how they know where the decimal point is to be placed.

3. Volunteers write the solutions for the unsolved problems on the board.

4. Discuss the rules for placing the decimal in each type of problem.

   • In addition and subtraction problems, the decimals are lined up and the decimal points are brought down to the answer.

   • In multiplication problems, count the numbers behind (to the right of) the decimal points. Beginning with the last number in the answer, count out that many places and place the decimal point in front of those numbers.

   • In division problems, place the decimal point in the answer space directly above its location in the dividend.

# Divide the Candy

by Tekla White

▶ **Materials:** overhead projector, wrapped hard candies, scrap paper, pencils

▶ **Here's How!**

1. Place a group of 10 candies on the overhead projector.

2. Tell students that they are going to use percents to figure how much of the candy they can receive.

3. Give a percentage.

4. Students write down the number of candies they would receive.

5. Students exchange papers and check each other's answers.

6. Repeat using a different number of candies.

7. Give everyone a share of the candy at the end of the activity.

# What's the Problem?

by Martha Cheney

▶ **Materials:** chalkboard, chalk, paper, pencils

▶ **Here's How!**

1. Write a number on the chalkboard.

2. Ask students to write on their papers as many problems as they can that have the given number as an answer.

   If desired, you may specify the operation. For example, you might give the number 96 and specify multiplication. (Possible problems are shown below.)

▶ **Variation**

Students write a set of four problems having the same answer (one problem for each operation), trade sets with a neighbor, and solve each other's problems. For example:

19 + 20, 156 − 117, 13 x 3, 1326 ÷ 34 (The answer to all four problems is 39.)

# Touchdown

by Ethel Condon

▶ **Materials:** chart paper, marker

▶ **Here's How!**

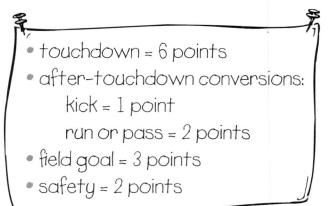

- touchdown = 6 points
- after-touchdown conversions:
     kick = 1 point
     run or pass = 2 points
- field goal = 3 points
- safety = 2 points

1. Ask the class to tell how points are scored in a football game. List these on a chart.

2. Then pose this question: How could a team score 23 points in a game? Work as a class to come up with several correct answers.

| | | | | | | | |
|---|---|---|---|---|---|---|---|
| 2 TD = | 12 | 3 TD = | 18 | 1 TD = | 6 |
| 1 R = | 2 | 1 S = | 2 | 1 R = | 2 |
| 1 K = | 1 | 1 FG = | 3 | 5 FG = | 15 |
| 4 S = | 8 | | 23 | | 23 |
| | 23 | | | | |

3. The next time you play, divide the class into partners or small groups. Use actual game scores if it's football season. Challenge students to come up with as many correct ways as they can to reach a score.

# Roll 'Em

by Ethel Condon

▶ **Materials:** three dice, paper, pencils

▶ **Here's How!**

1. Roll the dice.

2. Students write down a three-digit number using those numbers that land face up.

3. Roll the dice again. After each roll, students add the new three-digit number to the preceding total. The goal is to get closest to 2,000.

4. Roll the dice a total of five times.

5. After the first game, discuss strategies used to come close to 2,000. For example, if you have a total of 1,756 after three rolls and the fourth roll results in 5, 3, and 1 showing on the dice, what would be the best choice for a three-digit number? (135) Why? (You still have one roll to go and you are very close to 2,000 already.)

6. Play another game to see if students are able to use good strategies to come closer to the goal. (A savvy student may discover that with five rolls, you want to average 400 per roll to hit 2,000.)

▶ **Variations**

- Change the number of dice used. How will strategies change?

- Use four dice and have the students make two fractions and then add or subtract them.

- Increase the number of dice used. Students add the numbers they write for the first two rolls and then subtract the number from the third roll. Continue rolls, alternating operations.

# More Than I Needed to Know

by Delana Heidrich

▶ **Materials:** instructor's math textbook

▶ **Here's How!**

1. Practice determining what information in word problems is important by presenting problems with extraneous information. Read aloud a word problem from your math book. Add one unnecessary detail. (See sample problem below.)

2. Ask students to identify the extraneous information orally.

▶ **Variation**

Allow individual students to play the instructor role, reading word problems from the textbook and adding unimportant details.

Janet wants to bake cupcakes for 48 friends at her school. The recipe Janet is using yields 24 cupcakes. Five of the students in her class ride Janet's bus. By what number will Janet need to multiply the amounts listed in her recipe to make enough cupcakes to serve all of her friends?

# How Many?

by Tekla White

▶ **Materials:** overhead projector, paper, pencils

▶ **Here's How!**

1. Write the items at right, from the following story, on the overhead projector.

2. Read this story to the class.

> Five friends were invited to Clarence's birthday celebration. Clarence wanted to divide the party items evenly among his friends. Before Clarence divided the items, he set aside cupcakes and candy for himself, his parents, and his sister. There were 15 noisemakers, 5 yo-yos, 125 pieces of candy, and 10 cupcakes to divide among his friends. How much did Clarence give to each friend?

| | |
|---|---|
| 5 | people |
| 15 | noisemakers |
| 5 | yo-yos |
| 125 | pieces of candy |
| 10 | cupcakes |

3. Have students check their answers with a neighbor. Discuss answers as a group. Which part was the most difficult to solve? (125 pieces of candy) What strategies did students use in solving it?

4. Read the problem to students again. Ask them to raise their hands when they hear a sentence that does not help solve the problem.

> (Before Clarence divided the items, he set aside cupcakes and candy for himself, his parents, and his sister.)

| | |
|---|---|
| 3 | noisemakers |
| 1 | yo-yo |
| 25 | pieces of candy |
| 2 | cupcakes |

# What's Your Story?

by Jodee Mueller & David Gerk

▶ **Materials:** paper, pencils, chalkboard, chalk

▶ **Here's How!**

1. Write a number sentence on the chalkboard.

2. Direct students to write a word problem that could be solved by the number sentence.

3. Have students work a neighbor's word problem to make sure it illustrates the number sentence.

$5 \times 7 - 2 = 33$

$10 \times 6 \text{ divided by } 3 = 20$

$28 \times 4 + 3 = 115$

$15 + 25 \text{ divided by } 8 = 5$

▶ **Variations**

• Have students write their own number sentences and word problems to go with the sentences.

• Have students write word problems using information from units of study in science, social studies, etc.

The bus made five stops. Seven people got on at each stop. At the next stop, two people got off. How many people are on the bus?

# Darts
### by Martha Cheney

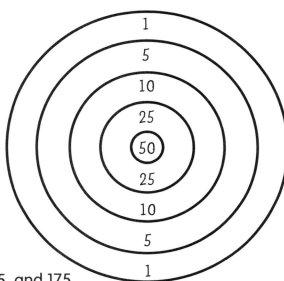

▶ **Materials:** chart paper and marker or chalkboard and chalk, paper, pencils

▶ **Here's How!**

1. Draw a simple dartboard on the chart paper or chalkboard.

2. Label each section of the dartboard with a number, as shown.

3. Ask students to find a way they could score a certain number of points using five "darts," assuming that every dart hits the target. (Sometimes, the score given may be impossible to achieve with five darts.)

4. Try these scores for starters: 67, 80, 100, 125, and 175.

▶ **Variations**

- Create a new dartboard using different numbers.
- Require a different number of darts.

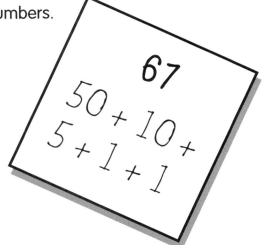

67
50 + 10 + 5 + 1 + 1

# Who's Place?
### by Ethel Condon

▶ **Materials:** overhead projector and transparency (see box below), paper, pencils

▶ **Here's How!**

1. In advance, prepare an open-ended overhead transparency. Use several or all of the items given below.

2. When you need it, pull out the transparency, fill in the blanks for a couple of items, and you're set.

3. Students answer as many items as time allows.

---

1. What is the smallest whole number you can make using the digits _____, _____, _____, and _____ ? Use each digit only once. Answer: _____

2. Which of the following represents the greatest number?
   1. three hundred and 60
   2. 300 + 40 + 9
   3. three hundred, fifty two
   4. 3 hundreds, 4 tens, 3 ones

3. In which of the following numbers does _(8)_ have the greatest value?
   1. 4820
   2. 5381
   3. 8652
   4. 3148

4. Make this number sentence true.
   _____ hundreds + _____ tens + _____ ones = _____

---

# Factor It In

by Laurie Williams

▶ **Materials:** none

▶ **Here's How!**

1. Have students count off by ones. Instruct them to remember their numbers.

2. Call out a multiplication number sentence, for example, 3 x 4 =. The answer may not be larger than the number of students.

3. The student whose number answers the problem (12) is to come to the front of the room.

4. Ask students who are factors of that number to also come to the front (1, 2, 3, 4, and 6).

▶ **Variation**

Give two products, for example, 16 and 24. Ask students whose numbers are factors of both products (common factors) to come to the front of the room (1, 2, 4, 8). Students state their numbers. The class confirms whether they are common factors. Ask the greatest common factor to raise his or her hand.

# Something in Common
by Jodee Mueller & David Gerk

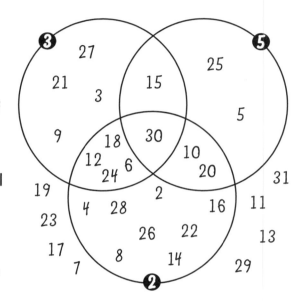

▶ **Materials:** large chart paper, marking pen

▶ **Here's How!**

1. In advance, draw a Venn diagram on the chart paper. Label the circles "Multiples of 2," "Multiples of 3," and "Multiples of 5."

2. Students count off starting with 2. For example, if there are 30 students, they will be numbered 2 through 31.

3. One at a time, students write their numbers in the appropriate section of the diagram. (If the number does not fit in any section, write it outside the diagram.)

4. After each student's turn, ask the class if the number is in the right place. If it's not, help the student correct it.

5. Read all the multiples for each number. What are the common multiples of 2 and 3? Of 3 and 5? 2 and 5? 2, 3, and 5?

6. Discuss any patterns you see. For example, prime numbers are outside the circles, 30 is the first number that is a common multiple of all three numbers, far more numbers fall in the "2" circle than in the other circles, etc.

▶ **Variations**

• Students count off again beginning with the next number in order, and then write these new numbers in the Venn diagram. Ask students to make some predictions about the results before they begin to place the numbers.

• Choose other sets of multiples for the Venn diagram.

# Count Down

by Tekla White

▶ **Materials:** soft ball or bean bag

▶ **Here's How!**

1. All students stand up.

2. Hand the ball to the first player. That student says "6" and tosses the ball to someone else.

3. The person catching the ball says the next multiple of 6 (12) and throws the ball to another student.

   When a player responds correctly, he or she may sit down after throwing the ball. If the student cannot name the next multiple, he/she throws the ball to another student, but remains standing.

4. The game continues until all the students are seated or no one can name the next multiple of 6.

▶ **Variation**

Students count by any number you wish.

# Take a Guess

by Ethel Condon

▶ **Materials:** chalkboard and chalk, paper, pencil

▶ **Here's How!**

1. Draw a labeled T chart on the chalkboard.

2. Write a number on a piece of paper.

3. Announce the range of the number to the class. Example: "My number is between 1 and 100."

4. Have individual students begin to guess. Write their guesses in the appropriate column until they get to your number.

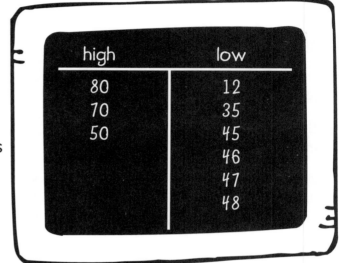

| high | low |
|------|-----|
| 80 | 12 |
| 70 | 35 |
| 50 | 45 |
|    | 46 |
|    | 47 |
|    | 48 |

5. Count how many tries it took to determine the number. Then discuss possible strategies to use to get to the number faster.

6. Play again as time allows.

49

# Number Crunchers

by Laurie Williams

▶ **Materials:** none

▶ **Here's How!**

1. Have students count off by ones. Instruct them to remember their numbers.

2. Give directions that are appropriate to concepts being studied. For example:

   • all of the prime numbers stand

   • all of the even numbers stand

   • all of the odd numbers stand

   • all numbers divisible by 1 stand (all stand)

   • all numbers that are multiples of 5 stand

3. Have students who stand state their numbers in order. Correct any wrong "numbers."

# Daily Numbers

by Martha Cheney

▶ **Materials:** scrap paper, pencils (optional)

▶ **Here's How!**

This is a fun way to reinforce numbers that we use in everyday life.

1. Call out a question that has a numerical answer. (See list below.)

2. Students may respond in a number of ways:

- raise their hands
- call out answers (if you are comfortable with a bit of noise)
- tell the answer to a neighbor
- write the answer on paper; exchange with a neighbor to check

**Sample Questions**

How many legs on a spider, a moose, an ant?
How many days in the month of (any month)?
How many days in a year?
How many hours in a day?
How many minutes in an hour?
How many seconds in a minute?
How many quarts in a gallon, cups in a pint, pints in a quart?
How many centimeters in a meter, meters in a kilometer?
How many keys on a piano, strings on a guitar?
How many planets in our solar system?
How many nickels, quarters, dimes, pennies in a dollar? In five dollars?
How many football, baseball, basketball players can play at one time?
How many corners on a triangle, square, pentagon, hexagon, octagon?

How many seasons in a year?
How many ounces in a pound?
How many senators from each state?
How many months in a year?
How many states in the U.S.?
How many stripes on the U.S. flag?
How many feet in a mile?
How many inches in a yard, a foot?
How many eggs in a dozen?

▶ **Variation**

Divide the class into two teams and play as a short trivia match. Allow 1 point for each correct answer.

# Now What?

by Ethel Condon

▶ **Materials:** chalkboard and chalk, or overhead projector and pen, paper, pencils

▶ **Here's How!**

1. On the chalkboard or overhead, write a string of numbers. Begin with simple sequences and progress to more difficult ones.

2. Ask the class to determine the pattern and supply the missing numbers.

3. Challenge students to write their own number strings and exchange them to solve each other's.

**Number Pattern Examples**

1, 2, 4, 8, _____, _____, _____  Pattern is × 2
5, 13, 21, 29, _____, _____, _____  Pattern is + 8
5, 7, 6, 8, 7, 9, 8, _____, _____, _____, _____  Pattern is + 2 , - 1
98, 93, 97, 92, 96, _____, _____, _____, _____  Pattern is - 5, + 4
41, 39, 40, 38, 39, 37, 38, _____, _____, _____  Pattern is - 2, + 1
10, 6, 18, 14, 26, 22, 34, _____, _____, _____  Pattern is - 4, + 12
4, 20, 100, 500, _____, _____, _____  Pattern is × 5

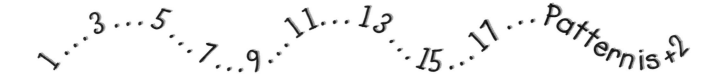

1...3...5...7...9...11...13...15...17...Pattern is +2

# What's the Pattern?

by Jodee Mueller & David Gerk

▶ **Materials:** overhead projector and pen, or chalkboard and chalk, paper, pencils

▶ **Here's How!**

1. Group students in pairs.

2. Write one number pattern on the overhead or chalkboard.

3. Pairs agree on the missing numbers and decide on what the pattern is.

4. Choose one pair to write the answer and tell the pattern.

5. Repeat using a new pattern.

**Patterns to Use**

| 10 | 5 |
|----|---|
| 6  | 3 |
| 16 |   |
| 40 |   |

| 4  | 45 |
|----|----|
| 7  | 75 |
| 10 |    |
| 22 |    |

| 30 | 15 |
|----|----|
| 17 | 2  |
| 50 |    |
| 67 |    |

| 50 | 10 |
|----|----|
| 5  | 1  |
| 40 |    |
| 75 |    |

| 25  | 5 |
|-----|---|
| 81  | 9 |
| 49  |   |
| 121 |   |

| 4  | 15 |
|----|----|
| 9  | 30 |
| 6  | 21 |
| 22 |    |

# Number Patterns

by Laurie Williams

▶ **Materials:** chalkboard and chalk, calculators (optional)

▶ **Here's How!**

1. Begin by orally giving the students numbers that follow a pattern.

2. Three students at a time come to the chalkboard. They each finish your pattern by writing the next three numbers that follow the same pattern.

3. When the students finish writing, ask one of them to tell what the pattern was.

4. Choose a student to think of a number pattern and give three to four numbers that follow the pattern.

**Examples**

| Numbers | Next three numbers | Pattern |
| --- | --- | --- |
| 2, 4, 8, 16 ____, ____, ____ | 32, 64, 128 | Multiplying by 2 |
| 100, 50, 25, ____, ____, ____ | 12.5, 6.25, 3.125 | Dividing by 2 |
| 7 ¾, 8 ½, 9 ¼, ____, ____, ____ | 10, 10 ¾, 11 ½ | Adding ¾ |
| 4, 9, 16, 25, ____, ____, ____ | 36, 49, 64 | Square of the next number |

# Small Change
### by Tekla White

▶ **Materials:** plain paper, pencils

▶ **Here's How!**

1. Divide students into groups of three or four.

2. Instruct each group to fold a piece of paper into eighths. Make additional paper available.

3. Read the following word problem to the students:

   > Elmo bought a yo-yo at the school flea market for 50 cents. He gave the person selling the yo-yo one dollar. The person making change had pennies, nickels, dimes, and quarters. How many different combinations of coins could Elmo receive in change? He can not receive more than five of any one coin.

4. Model how to show an answer by drawing circles and labeling them with a letter or money amount.

5. Challenge students to draw and write as many answers as they can. Write one solution in each box on the paper. Use additional paper as needed.

6. Call on students one at a time to post answers on a chart. Answers may not be repeated.

7. When students run out of answers, count the variations they discovered.

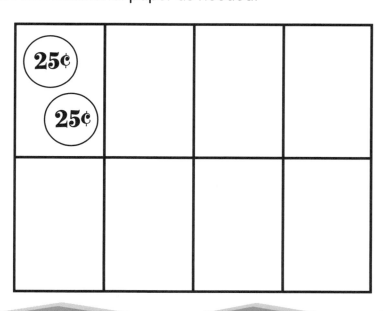

# How Do You Measure Up?

by Ethel Condon

▶ **Materials:** none

▶ **Here's How!**

1. Ask the students to think of two items at home that would be measured any of the following ways:

| | | | |
|---|---|---|---|
| inches | ounces | meters | gallons |
| feet | pounds | centimeters | quarts |
| yards | cups | millimeters | pints |

2. Students share answers with a neighbor.

3. Share several answers with the class. Discuss the reasoning for the answers given.

4. Continue with another unit of measurement.

▶ **Variation**

Play the game using other settings. Examples: school, movie theater, park.

# Boring Tunnels

## by Tekla White

▶ **Materials:** chart paper or transparency (see below), paper, pencils, calculators (optional)

▶ **Here's How!**

1. In advance, prepare a chart or transparency that contains the information at right.

2. Have students work individually or in pairs to answer the following questions:

   What is the difference in the length (in feet and/or in miles) between—

   Yerba Buena Island Tunnel and the Eisenhower Memorial Tunnel? (6,301 feet) (1.19 miles)

   Hitra Tunnel and the St. Gotthard Tunnel? (36,432 feet) (6.9 miles)

   Hitra Tunnel and the Yerba Buena Island Tunnel? (14,784 feet) (2.8 miles)

5,280 feet = 1 mile

Eisenhower Memorial Tunnel,
   Colorado—1.69 miles long
St. Gotthard Tunnel,
   Switzerland—10.12 miles long
Yerba Buena Island Tunnel,
   California—0.5 mile long
Hitra Tunnel,
   Norway— 3.3 miles long

## Variation

▶ Write the lengths of the tunnels in feet, and ask students to answer the same questions.

   Yerba Buena Island—2,640 feet

   Eisenhower Memorial—8,941 feet

   Hitra—17,424 feet

   St. Gotthard—53,856 feet

# Measuring Madness
by Delana Heidrich

▶ **Materials:** inch and centimeter rulers, common classroom items, chalkboard, chalk

▶ **Here's How!**

1. Select a common classroom item available to all students. For example, desktop, textbook, scissors, paper, or crayon.

2. Ask students to predict the length, width, or thickness of the item in both inches and centimeters. Record some of the predictions on the chalkboard.

3. Have students measure the item.

4. Report measurements in both inches and centimeters.

5. Compare the estimates with the actual measurements. Discuss the relationship of inches and centimeters.

▶ **Variations**

- Select teams. Ask each team to guess the measurement of the selected item. The team whose member made the closest prediction gains a point.

- Work with volume measurements. Have students predict the volume of various classroom containers in both ounces and milliliters.

2¼ inches wide? 433 centimeters long? 24 ½ inches tall? 67.30 centimeters across? 9 inches deep? 13 centimeters from here to there? How do inches and centimeters compare?

# I Spy

by Laurie Williams

▶ **Materials:** none

▶ **Here's How!**

1. You "spy" an object in the classroom.

2. Describe the object, using only geometric shapes and approximate height, length, width, radius, or diameter, in customary measurement or metric measurement.

3. Students guess what you have spied.

4. The student who spies the object may then take a turn to give clues.

I spy a rectangular solid that is about 30 centimeters long and 1 decimeter wide.

# Guess Again
## by Tekla White

▶ **Materials:** ruler, yardstick, or meterstick, a book, several rectangular or square objects, paper, pencils, overhead projector or chalkboard

▶ **Here's How!**

1. Show the ruler, the yardstick, or meterstick, and a book. Discuss the length of each measuring instrument.

2. Ask students to first estimate the length and the width of the book by simply **looking** at the book, the ruler, and the yardstick. Ask, "What would be an estimate of the perimeter of the book?"

3. Measure the perimeter to confirm the estimate.

4. Students pair up to estimate the perimeter of the other objects.

5. Choose several students to measure the actual perimeter of the objects and write the measurements on the chalkboard or overhead.

6. Students compare their estimates with the actual measurements and discuss their conclusions.

▶ **Variation**

If a scale is available, have students estimate the weight of 10 different objects.

# Measure for Measure
by Marilyn Evans

▶ **Materials:** overhead projector, marking pen

▶ **Here's How!**

1. With the class, brainstorm units of measure. Ask appropriate questions to elicit measurements that students do not offer. For example:

| | | | |
|---|---|---|---|
| inch | second | gallon | penny |
| feet | minute | quart | nickel |
| yard | hour | pint | dime |
| mile | week | cup | quarter |
| kilometer | month | milliliter | half-dollar |
| meter | year | liter | dollar |
| centimeter | decade | | |
| millimeter | century | | |

2. Write the following on the overhead projector:

_____  _____ s  in a _____

3. Tell students you are going to write a number in the first blank. They are to think of units of measurement that would fit in the other blanks. Write *12* in the blank and give this example:

_____12_____  \_\_\_\_inches\_\_\_\_  in a  _____foot_____

4. Use as many equivalencies from the box below as time allows. Encourage multiple answers to the same problem and challenge students to come up with new examples.

**Some Equivalencies to Use**

| | | | |
|---|---|---|---|
| 3 feet in a yard | 100 centimeters in a meter | 24 hours in a day | 2 cups in a pint |
| 36 inches in a yard | 1000 meters in a kilometer | 7 days in a week | 2 pints in a quart |
| 5280 feet in a mile | 60 seconds in a minute | 12 months in a year | 4 quarts in a gallon |

# In a Heartbeat

by Jodee Mueller & David Gerk

▶ **Materials:** paper, pencils, calculators (optional)

▶ **Here's How!**

1. Divide students into pairs or small groups.

2. Provide students with this information:

    Your heart beats about 70 times per minute.

3. Challenge students to find the answers to the following math problems:

    How many times would your heart beat per hour?

    How many times would your heart beat per day?

    How many times would your heart beat per week?

    How many times would your heart beat per month?

▶ **Variations**

- Have students figure how many times their heart has beat in their lifetime.

- Use the ages of parents, siblings, grandparents, etc., to figure heartbeats in a lifetime.

# Reasonable Responses
by Delana Heidrich

▶ **Materials:** instructor's math textbook

▶ **Here's How!**

1. Read a word problem from your textbook to the class. For example: "A $200.00 bookshelf is on sale for 20% off."

2. Then present to your class either the problem's actual solution or an unreasonable solution. For example, "On sale, the bookshelf costs $220.00."

3. Without giving students time to work out the problem, ask them to raise a hand if they believe your stated answer is a reasonable solution to the problem.

4. Discuss or model the thought processes that lead students to decide if the answer was reasonable.

5. Continue to read word problems and factual or fabricated answers, asking students to identify reasonable and unreasonable responses. Some answers should be close enough to be reasonable, although not correct.

6. Discuss the application of this practice to checking written math work.

▶ **Variations**

- Give three possible answers to each problem. One of the answers you announce should be a reasonable or correct solution, while the other two should be unreasonable responses. Instruct students to choose the correct response.

- Divide the class into teams and play a competitive version of Reasonable Responses by giving a point to the team that first identifies a problem's correct response.

# And the Winner Is...

by Ethel Condon

▶ **Materials:** chalkboard, chalk, stopwatch

▶ **Here's How!**

1. This activity involves the class making estimates of the time it will take to complete a silly task. Ask, "How long will it take to twiddle your thumbs forward 25 times and then backward 25 times?

2. Write the estimates on the chalkboard.

3. Ask a volunteer to perform the task.

4. Time the task using a stopwatch.

5. Record the actual time on the board. Compare it to the estimates.

6. Continue with other silly tasks. Does estimating proficiency improve? Discuss any strategies students are using to arrive at an estimate.

**Ideas for Other Silly Tasks**

• Do 10 sit-ups and then sing "Happy Birthday."
• Write all the 3 times tables to 60 on the chalkboard.
• Name 4 states and the name of our school.
• Snap your fingers 15 times.

**Tasks That Require Two People**

• Tie your shoelaces together. Hop 10 times.
• Sing alternating verses of a familiar song.
• List the first and last names of all the people in your family on a sheet of paper. Hand it to your partner to read aloud.

 Ten-Minute Activities for Grades 4–6 • EMC 785

# Square Feet
### by Tekla White

▶ **Materials:** chalkboard, chalk, paper, pencils, calculators (optional)

▶ **Here's How!**

1. Divide the class into groups of four students.

2. On the chalkboard, write the dimensions at right, for playgrounds.

3. Ask each group to write the problems on a piece of paper in order from the largest area in square feet to the smallest. Students must estimate to determine the order. They are not to calculate the answers.

4. After they have listed the problems, the groups multiply to find the answers, using paper and pencil or calculators.

5. The groups compare their lists to the actual square footage, making a corrected list if necessary.

6. Groups report the accuracy of their estimates. Discuss strategies used to complete the task.

$$28' \times 80' =$$
$$68' \times 38' =$$
$$36' \times 70' =$$
$$39' \times 67' =$$
$$41' \times 65' =$$

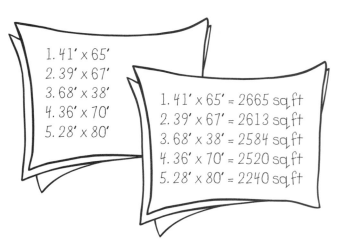

1. 41' x 65'
2. 39' x 67'
3. 68' x 38'
4. 36' x 70'
5. 28' x 80'

1. 41' x 65' = 2665 sq ft
2. 39' x 67' = 2613 sq ft
3. 68' x 38' = 2584 sq ft
4. 36' x 70' = 2520 sq ft
5. 28' x 80' = 2240 sq ft

# A Good Guess
### by Tekla White

▶ **Materials:** overhead projector and marker, or chalkboard and chalk, paper, pencils, calculators (optional)

▶ **Here's How!**

1. Write the problems at right on the overhead projector or chalkboard.

2. Students write the problems on their papers.

3. Direct students to estimate the answer by rounding off the dividends to the nearest hundreds or thousands, and the divisor to the nearest tens. If necessary, they should rewrite the problem in rounded-off form.

| | |
|---|---|
| 1. $9\overline{)703}$ | $10\overline{)700}$ |
| 2. $23\overline{)325}$ | $20\overline{)300}$ |
| 3. $67\overline{)2768}$ | $70\overline{)3000}$ |
| 4. $34\overline{)3322}$ | $30\overline{)3000}$ |
| 5. $58\overline{)588}$ | $60\overline{)600}$ |

4. As students work on their estimated answers, write the actual answers out of order on the overhead or chalkboard.

5. Direct students to select the answer that seems to be the best for each problem according to their estimates.

| Estimates | Answers |
|---|---|
| 1. 70 | 78.11 |
| 2. 15 | 14.13 |
| 3. 40 | 41.31 |
| 4. 100 | 97.71 |
| 5. 10 | 10.14 |

6. Discuss students' answers. Were the estimates larger or smaller than the answers? Why?

# Seeing Shapes

### by Marilyn Evans

▶ **Materials:** overhead transparency of figure below, pencils

▶ **Here's How!**

1.  You may wish to reproduce the figure below for individual students as well as on an overhead transparency.

2.  Challenge students to determine:

    • How many triangles?

    • What other shapes are there? How many of each?

**Answers**

There are 29 triangles.
There are 5 rectangles.
There are 5 parallelograms; 2 of these are rhombuses.
There are 2 trapezoids.

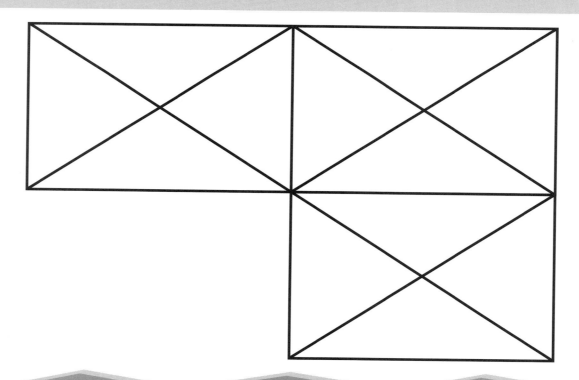

# Clock Watchers

by Laurie Williams, Jodee Mueller, David Gerk

▶ **Materials:** Judy® clock, chalkboard, chalk

▶ **Here's How!**

1. Remind students that angles may be classified as *acute* (less than 90 degrees), *obtuse* (more than 90 degrees), or *right* (90 degrees).

2. Position the hands of the clock at various times. Point to the section of the clock you wish to name.

   7:30   acute angle
   3:00   right angle
   12:20  obtuse angle

3. On the chalkboard, write:

   Acute—stand
   Obtuse—sit
   Right angle—kneel

1 o'clock
acute angle

9 o'clock
right angle

5 o'clock
obtuse angle

4. Show a number of times on the clock, pointing to the section to be named. Students respond by positioning themselves correctly. Whenever the response is not unanimously correct, discuss the answer.

| | | | |
|---|---|---|---|
| 5:45 obtuse angle | 3:55 obtuse angle | 7:55 obtuse angle | 6:40 acute angle |
| 9:00 right angle | 4:10 acute angle | 10:35 right angle | 12:15 right angle |
| 3:30 right angle | 9:20 obtuse angle | 12:05 acute angle | 2:20 acute angle |

# Shape Break
### by Tekla White

▶ **Materials:** rulers, compass, paper, pencils, crayons or marking pens

▶ **Here's How!**

1. Ask students to use their drawing tools to construct a circle or a rectangle in the center of their paper. This is the body for an imaginary animal robot.

2. Give students a specified amount of time to complete the robot using geometric shapes. They may not repeat the shapes for different body parts. For example, the ears may both be the same shape, but that shape may not be used again. The same rule applies to arms, legs, and eyes.

3. Compile a list of all the geometric shapes used. If there is time, graph the number of each shape used.

4. Students may color their robots.

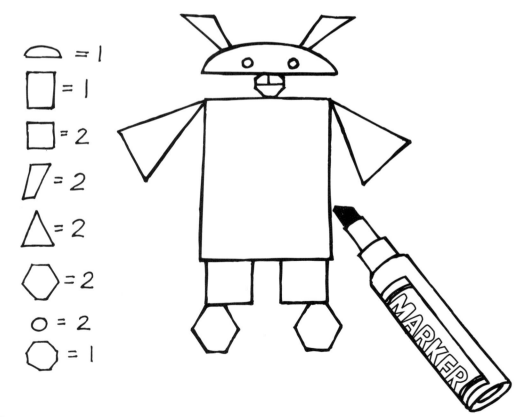

# Fraction Faction

by Jodee Mueller & David Gerk

▶ **Materials:** overhead projector or chart paper, marking pen

▶ **Here's How!**

1. Write the information at right on a chart or overhead projector.

2. Read the information with students.

3. Ask the following questions:

   - How many M&M's in the bag? (15)

   - What fraction of the M&M's are red?–(5/15 or 1/3) orange?–(2/15) blue?–(1/15) brown?–(3/15 or 1/5) yellow?–(4/15)

   - The red, orange, and brown M&M's together make up what fraction of the bag? (10/15 or 2/3)

   - What colors of M&M's could you put together to make 2/5 of the bag? (yellow & orange; or red & blue; or orange, blue, and brown)

   - What is the total number of pieces in a handful of trail mix? (24)

   - Which item makes up 1/4 of the trail mix?–(raisins) 1/6?–(dried fruit)

   - Which items together make up one more than half of the trail mix? (1/2 is 12; sunflower seeds + dried fruit = 13)

   - What fraction of the trail mix is raisins and dried fruit combined? (10/24 or 5/12)

   - What fraction of the trail mix is raisins and peanuts combined? (11/24)

In a bag of M&M's there are:

5 red M&M's,
2 orange M&M's,
1 blue M&M,
3 brown M&M's,
4 yellow M&M's

In a handful of trail mix there are:

6 raisins, 5 peanuts,
9 sunflower seeds,
4 pieces of dried fruit

# Fraction Action

by Martha Cheney

▶ **Materials:** overhead projector, small classroom objects (paper clips, erasers, etc.)

▶ **Here's How!**

1. Place several of one type of object on the screen of the projector. For example, six paper clips.

2. Ask several questions requiring students to determine a fractional part. For example:

   You may take (1/2, 1/3, 2/3, 5/6, etc.) of the paper clips. How many will you take?

3. Students respond by holding up the correct number of fingers.

4. Repeat with a different number of objects, allowing the use of other fractions. For example, eight objects—1/4, 3/4, 6/8, 1/2, 2/4.

   If students don't notice, point out equivalent fractions. For example:

   When you took 2/4, how many did you take? (4)

   When you took 1/2, how many did you take? (4)

   So 1/2 and 1/4 are the same. They are equivalent fractions.

▶ **Variation**

Place two types of objects on the projector. Ask questions that require a fraction as a response. For example:

There are four pencils and six erasers. What fraction of the items are pencils? (4/10) Can you name that fraction another way? (2/5)

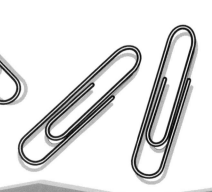

# Equal Parts

by Tekla White

▶ **Materials:** fraction cards, chalkboard and chalk, scratch paper, pencils

▶ **Here's How!**

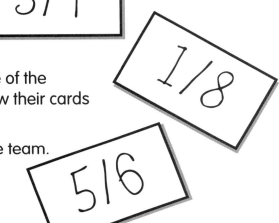

1. Review equivalent fractions if necessary.

2. Divide students into teams of five.

3. Students line up behind the leader.

4. Give the leader of each group one card with one of the fractions written on it. Tell the leaders not to show their cards to the other teams.

5. The leaders show their cards to the others on the team.

6. Give the teams several minutes to think of five equivalent fractions.

7. When you say, "Write," team members go to the chalkboard in relay fashion and write an equivalent fraction.

8. When a team has finished, members look at the fractions written on the board and work together to figure out the original fractions given to the other teams.

▶ **Variation**

Each student draws a fraction card from a box or bag and writes the fraction and an equivalent fraction on the board. The class checks the answers.

# Page Numbers
by Martha Cheney

▶ **Materials:** assorted books with varying numbers of pages, paper, pencils

▶ **Here's How!**

1. Hold up a book that has 48 pages.

2. Ask students to figure out how many page numbers include the numeral 3.

3. Allow use of paper and pencil the first time you try this.

4. Repeat the activity, using books with increasingly larger numbers of pages. After several experiences, are students able to make fairly accurate estimates without using paper and pencil?

▶ **Variation**

Choose any other numeral for the challenge.

# Guess Who?

by Delana Heidrich

▶ **Materials:** class roster copies, pencils

▶ **Here's How!**

1. Locate a student in your classroom who has an obvious unique feature. For example: purple shoes, birthday today, only student to get 100% on the last math test, etc. Students will use logic to help them determine who you have selected.

2. Distribute one class roster to each student.

3. Give students hints about the person you have selected. For example, "This person is not wearing jeans today." OR "This person sits in the front half of the room."

4. After each hint, instruct students to cross out the names on their class roster that do not meet the criteria of the hint.

5. Continue providing hints until only one name remains on the class roster.

▶ **Variations**

• Allow individual students a chance to play the teacher role, selecting a student and verbalizing clues. Suggest to the student that he or she keep track on his or her own roster the results of each clue provided.

• Determine what a preselected group of students have in common according to your clues, which will eliminate all other students from that group.

# Magic Squares

by Jodee Mueller & David Gerk

▶ **Materials:** copy paper with 3 x 3 grid, 2" squares of paper, pencils

▶ **Here's How!**

Magic squares can be frustrating when students have to write and erase numbers. Moving around numbered squares is more fun.

1. Reproduce a 3 x 3 grid for each pair of students.

2. Give each pair nine paper squares. They are to number the squares 1 through 9.

3. Students attempt to arrange the numbers on the grid so that each row, column, and both diagonals add up to 15.

4. Discuss strategies that seemed to work.

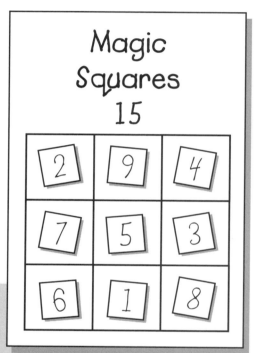

Magic Squares 15

| 2 | 9 | 4 |
| 7 | 5 | 3 |
| 6 | 1 | 8 |

**How to Make a Magic Square**
Write the middle-most (median) number in the center. On one diagonal write the numbers that are one more and one less than the median. On the other diagonal write the numbers that are three more and three less than the median. Now the rest are easy to fill in.

# Grand Graphing

by Laurie Williams

▶ **Materials:** chalkboard, chalk, paper, pencils, crayons, ruler

▶ **Here's How!**

1. Take a poll to find every student's shoe size.

2. Write the information on the chalkboard.

3. Using the above information, students graph the class's shoe sizes on a bar graph.

▶ **Variations**

- Graph other things:

  Shirt color (pattern or solid), favorite school lunch, birth months, city or state of birth, brothers, sisters, birth order, favorite school subject, hair length (long, short, medium), hair color, shoes (laces, Velcro®, slip-ons), allergies, colors of family cars

- Using the information gathered, have students show the data using fractions (e.g., 6/22 students wear a size 5 shoe) or decimals, by dividing the denominator into the numerator.

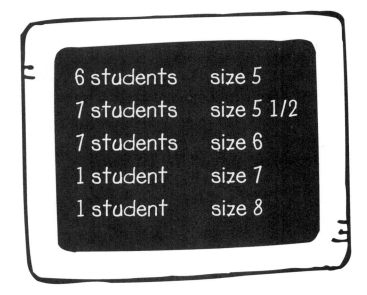

6 students       size 5
7 students       size 5 1/2
7 students       size 6
1 student        size 7
1 student        size 8

# Dealing with Data

by Delana Heidrich

▶ **Materials:** chalkboard, chalk, graph paper, pencils

▶ **Here's How!**

1. Present your students with a multiple-choice opinion question. For example, "Would you rather win a contest that offered a new car, a trip to Europe, or a month off from school?"

2. Record on the chalkboard students' names and corresponding responses.

3. Now challenge students to chart or graph responses to answer questions you present based on the information. Assign each question to a different group of students. For each question you ask, the groups will need to draw a different chart or graph. For example:

   • Do boys or girls prefer the trip to Europe?

   • Do students wearing blue jeans prefer to win the car?

   • What percentage of students chose a month off from school?

4. Compare the results and discuss how responses to the initial question need to be grouped together differently to answer specific questions.

▶ **Variations**

   • Rather than allowing students to choose their charting or graphing method, require them to use a method you are studying in class—pie charts, bar graphs, or line graphs.

   • Require students to make logical conclusions based on the responses of classmates to the question presented.

   • In addition to your asking questions, direct each student to devise three questions that could be answered using the data collected.

# Skyscrapers
by Martha Cheney

▶ **Materials:** calculators, yardstick

▶ **Here's How!**

1. Inform students that the Empire State Building is 1,250 feet tall.

2. Ask the class to determine how many students would have to stand one on top of the other to reach the top.

3. Measure the heights of several students and find the average.

4. Depending on the ability and experience of your students, round to the nearest foot or nearest inch and divide into the height of the building.

▶ **Variations**

* Repeat the process at another time using these buildings, or use buildings in your local area.

     Sears Tower  1,450 feet

     World Trade Center  1,368 feet

     Eiffel Tower  984 feet

* Repeat the process using metric measure for students and buildings.

     Empire State Building  381 meters

     Sears Tower  442 meters

     World Trade Center  417 meters

     Eiffel Tower  300 meters

# What's in a Name?

by Martha Cheney

▶ **Materials:** chart or list of students' first names, calculators, paper, pencils

▶ **Here's How!**

1. Give students a class list.

2. Ask students to:

   - find the average (mean) number of letters in the students' first names

   - find which letter or letters appear most frequently (mode)

   - determine the ratio of vowels to consonants, expressed as a fraction and as a percentage

▶ **Variation**

Try the same activity using last names. Compare the results.

| Tom | Chris | Matt |
| Susie | Will | Mary |
| Anna | Baron | Hannah |
| Ray | Carlo | Colton |
| George | Eva | Jamie |
| Holly | Pamela | Sue Ellen |
| Cristy | Joe | Karen |
| Claire | Paul | Daniel |

# Head Count

by Jodee Mueller & David Gerk

▶ **Materials:** small sticky notes, pencils, chalkboard, chalk

▶ **Here's How!**

1. Have each student write on a sticky note the number of people who live in his or her home (including the student).

2. Say, "We are going to use this information to make a bar graph on the chalkboard." Decide as a class whether the bars will be horizontal or vertical.

3. Write the labels for the rows (or columns) on the board (2 through 10 or more).

4. Beginning with the smallest household (2), students place their sticky notes on the board.

5. Work with the class to come up with the mean, median, and mode for the information graphed.

▶ **Variation**

Instead of family members, use the number of pets. Have students transfer the information to graph paper, being sure to label the axes and title the graph.

# Alike and Different

by Ethel Condon

▶ **Materials:** chalkboard, chalk

▶ **Here's How!**

1. Draw a Venn diagram on the chalkboard.

2. Label each circle as shown.

3. Have several students at a time write their names in the diagram where they apply. If both apply, the name should be written in the middle. If neither apply, the name should be written outside the circles.

4. Have students either verbalize or write down their findings. Encourage use of math vocabulary words.

   *There are more people in our class that have a dog than drink Pepsi.*

   *Seven people don't drink Pepsi or have a dog.*

# What's the Chance?

by Delana Heidrich

▶ **Materials:** chalkboard, chalk, a die

▶ **Here's How!**

1. Show a die. Ask students, "If you are rolling one die, what is the chance of rolling a 1?" Give students a chance to respond.

2. Then say, "Instead of the word *chance* we could use the word *probability*. *Probability* is the ratio of the number of likely outcomes to the total number of possible outcomes. Because there are six numbers on a die, it is likely that I will roll a 1 only one time out of every six rolls. So I say that the probability of rolling a 1 is 1 in 6. I can write it as 1/6."

3. Ask students the following questions:

   • Would the probability be the same for rolling any other number with one die? (yes)

   • With a probability of 1/6, how many times should you get each number if you rolled a die 60 times? (10)

4. Draw a chart on the board to use in recording the results.

| Number rolled | 1 | 2 | 3 | 4 | 5 | 6 |
|---|---|---|---|---|---|---|
| Tally | 卌 II | 卌 卌 I | 卌 卌 II | 卌 卌 | 卌 卌 II | 卌 III |
| Total times rolled | 7 | 11 | 12 | 10 | 12 | 8 |

5. Let students take turns rolling the die one time until 60 rolls have been made. Record the results of each roll on the chart.

6. Discuss any difference in your student's results and the probability ratio of 1/6. Why might this occur? (Probability is an estimate of the likelihood of an event, not a concrete number.)

# Coin Toss

### by Martha Cheney

▶ **Materials:** chart paper and marker, coin

▶ **Here's How!**

1. Create two columns labeled "heads" and "tails" on the chart paper.

2. Ask one or more volunteers to flip a coin 10 times.

3. Tally the results. Date the entry.

4. Repeat the process whenever you have a few spare minutes.

5. Discuss the idea of probability.

   • Does one episode of the coin toss always result in a 50/50 split?

   • What happens to the totals as you increase the number of episodes?

|  | heads | tails |
|---|---|---|
| Jan 4 | 卌 l | llll |
| Jan 12 | 卌 | 卌 lll |
| Feb 6 | l | 卌 卌 lll |
| Feb 28 | llll | 卌 卌 l |
| Mar 9 | lll | 卌 ll |
| Mar 13 | ll | 卌 lll |

▶ **Variations**

• Roll a die and keep track of the results in the same fashion.

• Roll two dice and keep track of the sums. Which sum appears most frequently? Why?

# The Mighty Mississippi
by Tekla White

▶ **Materials:** wall map, map of the United States for each group, paper, pencils

▶ **Here's How!**

1. Introduce the Mississippi River and show its source.

2. Explain that it isn't the longest river in the United States, but it discharges more water than any other river in the U.S. Many other rivers are tributaries of the Mississippi. That means they flow into or join the Mississippi River.

3. Divide students into groups of two or three, or students may work independently.

4. Ask students to make a list of states that have the Mississippi River as a border. Students use maps to find the answer.

| Answers | | | | |
|---|---|---|---|---|
| Arkansas | Illinois | Iowa | Kentucky | Louisiana |
| Minnesota | Mississippi | Missouri | Tennessee | Wisconsin |

▶ **Variation**

Ask students to name as many tributaries of the Mississippi as they can. Students compare their lists.

**Possible Answers**
Arkansas   Des Moines   Illinois   Minnesota   Missouri   Ohio   Red   Wisconsin
(students may locate and name smaller tributaries as well)

# Just the Facts
by Tekla White

▶ **Materials:** a number of items labeled with the name of the country in which they were made, world maps or atlases, encyclopedias, world almanacs, or other resource books, index cards

▶ **Here's How!**

1. Divide students into groups of four or fewer.

2. Each group selects an item from the box.

3. Students write the name of the country on an index card and locate the country on a world map.

4. Students find two facts about the country and write them on the card.

5. Groups may share the location of the country and the two facts with the class or post the information for others to read.

▶ **Variation**

Each group takes five items from the box and locates the countries where the items were made. They then mark the locations on the wall map.

Canada
1. Largest North American country
2. Divided into provinces

Italy
1. Shaped like a boot
2. Capital is Rome

# Work, Work, and More Work
by Tekla White

▶ **Materials:** paper, pencils, chalkboard and chalk, or chart paper and marker

▶ **Here's How!**

1. Students work in groups of four or fewer.

2. Give students 5 minutes to write the names of different kinds of jobs.

3. Each group, in order, names one of the jobs on its list until the group runs out of names. Compile a composite list on the chalkboard or a chart. Each job should be written only once.

4. The last group to name a job is the winner.

5. If time allows, or during another 10-minute period, have each group develop categories and classify the jobs on the composite list. Categories may be broad, such as "physical jobs" and "desk jobs," or more specific, such as "technology jobs," "building trade jobs," and "hospitality industry jobs."

cook
banker
truck driver
teacher
plumber
programmer
pilot
doctor

# Letters and States
by Tekla White

▶ **Materials:** paper, pencils, political maps of the United States

▶ **Here's How!**

1. Tell students to divide the paper into two columns and head them as shown below.

2. Students list the states in the appropriate columns.

**Answers**

The letter **a** twice: California, Nevada, Arizona, Montana, North Dakota, South Dakota, Nebraska, Oklahoma, Kansas, Louisiana, South Carolina, North Carolina, Maryland, Delaware, Pennsylvania, Indiana, Hawaii, Massachusetts

The letter **a** three times: Arkansas, Alaska

▶ **Variations**

- Students find and record all the states that begin with the word *New*. (Answers: New Mexico, New Hampshire, New Jersey, New York)

- Students find and record all the states that begin with one of the four directions. (Answers: North Carolina, South Carolina, North Dakota, South Dakota, West Virginia)

| 2 letter a | 3 letter a |
|------------|------------|
| California | Arkansas |
| Kansas | Alaska |
| Delaware | |
| Arizona | |
| Montana | |
| Nebraska | |
| Hawaii | |
| Maryland | |
| Oklahoma | |
| Indiana | |
| Nevada | |

# I'm on My Way

by Tekla White

▶ **Materials:** paper, pencils

▶ **Here's How!**

1. Divide students into groups of four or fewer.

2. Tell students to imagine that they will be moving to a new country tomorrow. Ask each group to list 10 items that they as a group would choose to take with them to help them survive.

3. Post the items suggested by each group.

4. Encourage students to discuss and compare the lists.

▶ **Variation**

Ask student groups to list 10 items they would take with them if they were going to a new planet. Post and discuss the answers.

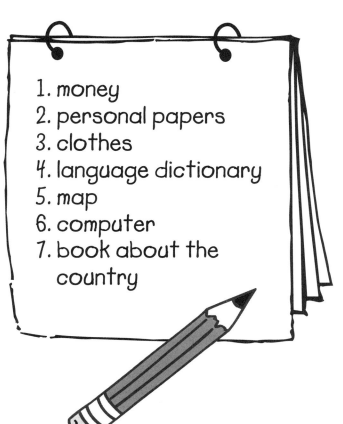

1. money
2. personal papers
3. clothes
4. language dictionary
5. map
6. computer
7. book about the country

# Schoolwood Squares

by Delana Heidrich

▶ **Materials:** lists of nine history or geography questions, chalkboard, chalk

▶ **Here's How!**

1. In advance, compile several lists of nine questions each from history or geography studies.

2. Draw a large square on the chalkboard. Divide it into nine smaller squares. Number the squares at random, 1 through 9. As in the television game show *Hollywood Squares*, students attempt to get tic-tac-toe by answering the questions correctly.

3. Divide students into two teams—X's and O's. Direct one member of the X team to select a numbered square.

4. Read the question you have assigned to that number. If the X team member answers the question correctly, mark an X in the square. If the answer is wrong, leave the square blank.

5. Next, direct one member of the O team to select a numbered square. Read the question assigned to that square. If the O team member answers correctly, mark an O in that square.

6. Continue play until one team has achieved tic-tac-toe.

▶ **Variations**

• As a good way to review for an upcoming test, have students create the questions to be used in Schoolwood Squares.

• Have teams collaborate on responses.

• Conduct a Schoolwood Squares tournament in which individual students (rather than teams) compete against one another until a champion is determined.

# Name That State!

by Delana Heidrich

▶ **Materials:** states written on sheets of paper, marker

▶ **Here's How!**

1. In advance, write the names of several states on several sheets of paper.

2. Divide the class into two teams.

3. Choose one player from each team to be IT. The ITs stand at the front of the room.

4. Walk in front of the rest of your students holding up a state name so that the ITs cannot see it.

5. Members of the two teams alternately give one- to two-word clues to their IT team member until one of the ITs guesses the state. For example, if you displayed the state *Nebraska* to your class, team members' clues might include "plains," "corn producers," or "Lincoln."

▶ **Variations**

- Play the game with vocabulary words from geography such as *mountain* and *ravine* or with names of battles or famous men and women from history.

- Students write complete paragraphs describing various countries, states, or regions studied. Other students guess the locations described.

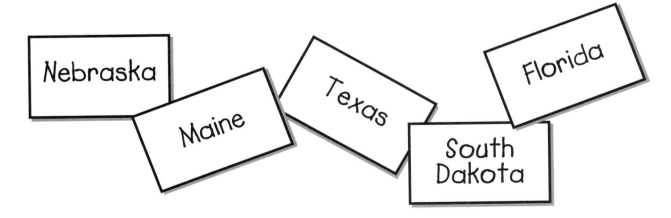

# City Planners

by Delana Heidrich

▶ **Materials:** paper, pencils, chart paper

▶ **Here's How!**

1. Divide students into groups of three to five.

2. Challenge each group to develop a list of the essential aspects of a city (infrastructure). Get them started by posing this problem:

   You are going to build a new city. Nothing is there now except bare land. What are the necessary structures you would have to construct so that the people in your city can function? Would there need to be roads? Absolutely! You have (time period) to list the things that are necessary to have a working city.

3. After the allotted time, compile groups' lists into one list. Evaluate the list, crossing out any nonessential items (movie theatres, donut shops, etc.).

4. Give students a chance to add more items to the list, then ask questions to help them add any infrastructure aspects that may have been left out.

   If a person in your city flushed a toilet in his or her home, would the water and waste have a place to go? (Your city needs a sewage system.)

   If a home in your city were on fire, could the fire be quickly contained? (Your city needs a fire department.)

# Life-Altering Inventions

by Delana Heidrich

▶ **Materials:** chalkboard, chalk, paper, pencils

▶ **Here's How!**

1. Have students fold their papers in half to form two columns, heading them "Positive" and "Negative."

2. On the chalkboard, write one of the life-altering inventions given in the box below. Ask students to write the positive and negative effects of the invention.

3. After 8 minutes, ask students to decide whether the invention would alter their lives and whether the change would be positive or negative.

| Positive | Negative |
|----------|----------|
|          |          |

flying car
diet machine
heal-all-diseases pill
personality-changing machine

automatic homework machine
time-traveling machine
five-second meal cooker

▶ **Variations**

• Have students design their own life-altering inventions.

• Assign a position to students and have them debate whether an invention would be positive or negative.

# Concerned Citizens

by Delana Heidrich

▶ **Materials:** chalkboard, chalk

▶ **Here's How!**

1. With students' help, list things that are working in your classroom or school and things that could use improvement.

2. Focus on one legitimate complaint. Devise a realistic plan for improvement.

3. Develop a time line for your plan.

▶ **Variations**

Explain that being a concerned citizen of a community and a nation extends beyond voting for effective leaders. Concerned citizens of communities plant flowers, build playgrounds, clean highways, organize summer art programs for youth, band together in neighborhood watch programs, and otherwise work to honor the good and improve the less effective aspects of their communities.

• List things being done by citizens in your community. Write notes of appreciation to the citizens responsible.

• Think of a problem in your community. Develop a plan to improve the situation. Participate in the plan.

Problem:
Our playground is littered.
Solutions:
1. Pick up litter.
2. Empty garbage cans more often.
3. Assign each class a "pick-up week."

# Keeping Our Home Planet Happy

by Delana Heidrich

▶ **Materials:** chalkboard, chalk, paper, pencils, chart paper

▶ **Here's How!**

1. Divide students into small groups.

2. Give each group one sheet of paper and instruct them to fold and label it as shown.

3. Write the statement "Styrofoam®️ is not biodegradable" on the chalkboard.

4. Ask students,

   - Where do you see Styrofoam being used?
   - What is it used for?
   - What could be used in place of Styrofoam in each instance?

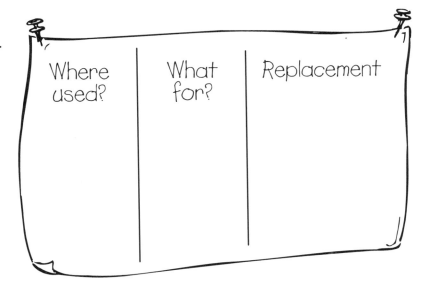

5. Give the groups 5 minutes to brainstorm and list responses to the three questions.

6. Compile the responses of all groups. Summarize the discussion with a recommendation for limiting the use of Styrofoam.

▶ **Variation**

Follow the steps above using different topics.

1. The production of paper relies on the cutting down of trees.

   - Name the uses of paper.
   - Give specific examples of ways paper use can be reduced.

2. Fresh water is becoming scarce in some places.

   - Why is fresh water important?
   - Where do we get fresh water?
   - How can water be conserved?

# Chronologically Challenged

by Delana Heidrich

▶ **Materials:** sets of three historical events on an overhead transparency or chart paper, paper, pencils

▶ **Here's How!**

1. In advance, compile a number of sets of three historical events taken from class studies. List each set of events out of chronological order on an overhead transparency or chart paper.

2. Divide the class into small groups. Groups appoint one student to serve as the recorder.

3. Show a set of events. Groups have 1 minute to write the events in chronological order. Groups raise their hands as they finish.

4. Groups receive a point if the events are correctly ordered. An extra point is given to the first group who answers correctly.

Battle of Fort Sumter

Lincoln assassinated

Emancipation Proclamation

▶ **Variation**

Have each group list sets of events out of chronological order. Rotate the lists from group to group.

# A Brief Moment of Fame

by Delana Heidrich

▶ **Materials:** chalkboard, chalk, encyclopedias, index cards, pencils

▶ **Here's How!**

1. As students distribute one volume from a set of encyclopedias and an index card to each student, write the information at right on the chalkboard.

2. Direct each student to locate a single-paragraph listing on a lesser-known person from history.

3. Students read the paragraph, find the information requested, and write it on the index card.

person's name
dates lived
country lived in
important thing
the person did

4. Students tell a neighbor about the person they have researched. If time allows, have students share some personalities with the class.

5. Place the index cards where interested students can read them in spare moments. You may want to post some search questions that challenge students to locate a particular individual. For example: Who was the person who lived at the time of the American Revolution?

▶ **Variation**

Name a person found in the class's history text and make a true or false statement about the individual. Students locate the person using the index and skim the information to verify the statement. Allow a reasonable amount of time and then let students show thumbs up or thumbs down to indicate whether your statement was true or false.

# Flying Our Flag

by Delana Heidrich

▶ **Materials:** butcher paper, drawing paper, markers

▶ **Here's How!**

1. In advance, divide a large piece of butcher paper into sections. There should be a section for each student and one for yourself. You may want to add a few additional sections to accommodate new students. Cut drawing paper the same size as these sections.

2. Explain to the class that a country's (or state's/province's) flag displays symbols that represent aspects of that place. Discuss the significance of the symbols on your nation's or state's/province's flag as an example. Tell students that they are going to help create a class flag that will display the diversity of each member of the class.

3. Give each student a piece of precut drawing paper.

4. Students are to draw something that symbolizes themselves (e.g., a book with their name on it, a soccer ball, a skateboard, a math equation, a paintbrush, a musical instrument, etc.).

5. Glue each completed drawing to a section of the butcher paper. Proudly display the class flag.

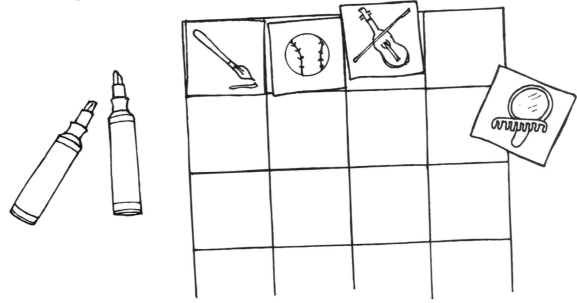

# Garbage Diggers

by Delana Heidrich

▶ **Materials:** artifact bags (see box below), paper, pencils

▶ **Here's How!**

1. In advance, put "artifacts" in bags or boxes. There should be one artifact container for every four or five students.

2. Divide the class into groups of four or five.

3. Explain that anthropologists use information gathered from ruins to make conclusions about past cultures. Explain that each group is going to draw conclusions about a person based on the items the group has "found."

4. Give each group a set of artifacts.

5. Groups are to examine each artifact and generate a list of conclusions or a hypothesis that might be drawn about the person who used them. For example, after viewing the first set of artifacts below, a group might conclude the following:

   - the person is really "into" electronics
   - the person has technology skills
   - the person uses the Internet
   - the person has access to a computer and a printer
   - the person likes to play games
   - the Gameboy® makes it more likely the person is male
   - the person's computer is not an old one because it has a CD drive

6. Groups then share their artifacts and conclusions with the class.

---

**Possible Sets of Artifacts**

| | |
|---|---|
| CD-ROM | golf ball |
| page printed from a Web site | swim goggles |
| headphones | sports section of newspaper |
| battery | TV schedule with ESPN highlighted |
| baseball card | tennis ball |
| Gameboy® | |

---

# Where's It Coming From?

by Ethel Condon

▶ **Materials:** daily newspaper, paper, pencils, chalkboard and chalk, or chart paper and marker

▶ **Here's How!**

1. Divide students into groups of three.

2. Assign jobs. Two students are the information searchers. The other student is the information recorder.

3. Allow 5 minutes for the searchers to look through the newspaper to find locations (continents, countries, states or provinces, cities) where news events took place. The recorder makes a list.

4. Recorders from each group report the results. Compile a class list on the chalkboard or chart paper.

5. Pose questions such as:

   How many different continents had a story in the news?
   How many different countries had stories in the paper?
   How many different states had stories in the paper?

# Charades

by Ethel Condon

▶ **Materials:** index cards with social studies-related words/phrases

▶ **Here's How!**

1. In advance:

   - Write social studies-related vocabulary words or phrases on the index cards. The first time you play, pick no more than two categories, for example, people and countries. Expand the categories as students become more proficient (historical objects such as the Santa Maria, events such as the Boston Tea Party, historical periods such as the Westward Movement).

   - Determine the clues students will use to identify the category. For example, a country could be a small "c" formed with the fingers; a person could be indicated by the student pointing to him or herself.

2. Explain the rules of Charades.

   - the object is to guess what the person is trying to act out

   - actors may not speak aloud; only gestures may be used

   - explain the clues used to tell the category in which the word or phrase fits

3. A student draws a card and attempts to act out the word or phrase while the others make guesses. (If your students have never played Charades, you should be prepared to do the acting the first few times.)

▶ **Variation**

As students become proficient at Charades, divide the class into teams. Stage two teams in several places in the classroom to allow more frequent participation.

# Location Station

## by Ethel Condon

▶ **Materials:** world, U.S., or state wall map, chalkboard, chalk

▶ **Here's How!**

1. Divide the class into two teams.

2. Use the appropriate wall map. All students should be able to view the map.

3. Select one student from each team. They stand in front of the map, facing the class.

4. Ask a location question appropriate to your area of study. For example:

   Can you find Indiana?
   Where's the Nile River?
   Point to the capital of Colorado.

5. The student who locates the answer first earns a point for his or her team. Keep a tally on the chalkboard.

6. Call a new student from each team to the map.

7. At the end of the playing period, the team with the most points is the winner.

# Let's Get Physical

by Ethel Condon

▶ **Materials:** index cards with physical features, chalkboard, chalk, atlas for each group, physical world wall map

▶ **Here's How!**

1. In advance, write the name of a physical feature on each index card. (See box below.) Use only those features that have been studied previously.

2. Divide students into groups of two or three.

3. Draw a card, read the physical feature, and write it on the chalkboard.

4. Each group locates an example of that physical feature in the atlas and raises their hands when they have done so.

5. After a reasonable time, allot one point to each group that has found the feature and an additional point to the first correct group.

6. Call a member of each group to the wall map to name and locate the specific example of the feature they found.

**Examples of Physical Features**

| plateau | river | island | bay | gulf | hills | mountains |
| channel | sea | strait | cape | highlands | valley | peninsula |
| ocean | lake | sound | delta | ice shelf | glacier | island group |
| point | inlet | reef | falls | volcano | mount | archipelago |

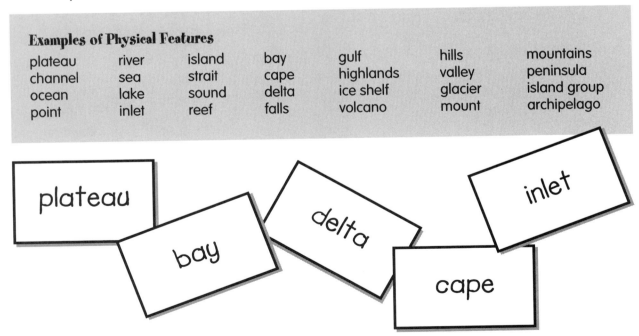

# The Match Game

by Ethel Condon

▶ **Materials:** index cards with geography words and definitions, world map

▶ **Here's How!**

1. In advance, write geography vocabulary words on one set of index cards. On a second set, write the definitions of those words. There should be one card for each student.

2. Distribute the cards to the class randomly.

3. Have one student begin by reading his or her card.

4. The student with the matching card responds by reading his or her card, and then both students collaborate to point to the place on the map.

5. Continue until all cards have been matched up.

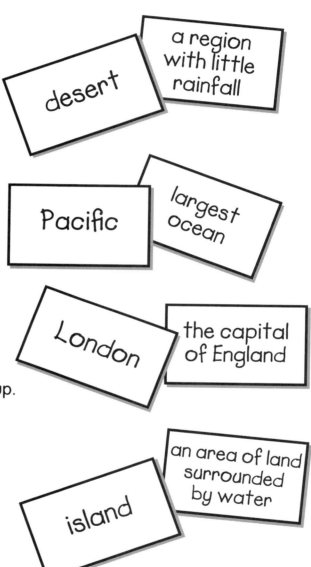

desert

a region with little rainfall

Pacific

largest ocean

London

the capital of England

island

an area of land surrounded by water

# Which Way Do I Go?

by Ethel Condon

▶ **Materials:** political maps for each group, world wall map, chalkboard, chalk

▶ **Here's How!**

1. Divide students into pairs or small groups. On the chalkboard, write the names of the members of each group for scoring purposes.

2. Call out two countries, cities and states, etc. For example:

   Which way do I go to get from San Francisco, California, to New Orleans, Louisiana?

   Which way do I go to get from Saudi Arabia to India?

3. Groups locate the two places on their map and discuss the direction they would travel.

4. A member of each group goes to the board and writes the direction (e.g., N, SE, etc.).

5. Each team with a correct answer receives a point. The first correct team receives an additional point.

# Where in the World?

by Ethel Condon

▶ **Materials:** wall map or student atlases

▶ **Here's How!**

1. Predetermine a place in your state/province, country, or the world.

2. Challenge the class to figure out your location. Explain that you are going to help by giving clues that begin with general information, and that each additional clue will be more specific. (See examples in box below.)

3. Initially, after each clue, discuss the possible answers. This helps the students understand the process of going from general to specific.

4. Keep giving clues until someone has the answer.

5. Start simple and move to more complex clues.

6. Eventually, students may write their own sets of clues.

**Belize**

1. I'm in the Northern Hemisphere.
2. I'm in North America.
3. I'm north of the Panama Canal.
4. I border the Caribbean Sea.
5. I'm south of Mexico.
6. My other neighbor is Guatemala.

**Nile River**

1. I'm one of the longest rivers in the world.
2. I'm in an African country.
3. I'm north of the equator.

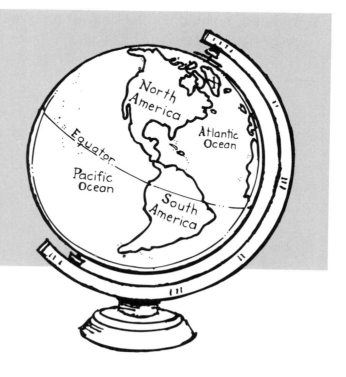

# What Time Is It?

by Ethel Condon

▶ **Materials:** U.S. map with time zones

▶ **Here's How!**

1. Review or clarify the concept that the U.S. is divided into time zones. As one moves west, the time is one hour earlier in each time zone.

2. Name two states. For example, Florida and Nevada.

3. Ask, "Is it earlier or later in Florida than in Nevada?"

4. Reverse the question.

5. Move on to specific times. For example:

   If it's 4:00 a.m. in New York, what time is it in Nevada?

   What time is it in Phoenix if it is noon in Los Angeles?

▶ **Variation**

Let students pose questions for the class to answer.

# A-B-C

by Ethel Condon

▶ **Materials:** textbooks (optional), overhead projector or chart paper

▶ **Here's How!**

1. Divide students into small groups. Number the groups to track the order in which they are to participate.

2. Call out a continent, country, group of people, or an event being studied. For example:

| | | |
|---|---|---|
| Australia | Germany | Ute Indians |
| Gold Rush | Revolutionary War | George Washington |

3. Instruct the students to think alphabetically about that particular place, person, or event. They may use reference books.

4. Group 1 is to call out a word or phrase beginning with *A* that relates to the subject. Give the group a specified amount of time (15 seconds) to confer.

5. Group 2 must think of a word or phrase beginning with *B*, and so on. If a group does not have a word or phrase at the end of the allotted time, they are to say "Pass." The next group attempts to use that letter.

6. Record the results on chart paper or on an overhead transparency.

## Topic–Australia

| | | |
|---|---|---|
| **A**yer's Rock | **j**umping kangaroos | **S**nowy Mountains |
| **B**risbane | **k**oalas | **T**asmania |
| capital is **C**anberra | **L**ord Howe Island | **U**luru is the Aboriginal name |
| "**d**own under" | many **m**arsupials | for Ayer's Rock |
| **e**ucalyptus forests | **N**ew South Wales | **v**egemite is a spread Australians |
| **F**raser Island | **o**pals are mined | put on bread |
| **G**reat Barrier Reef | **P**erth is in western Australia | **w**allabies are like small kangaroos |
| **h**omesteads | **q**uokka | **y**achting in Sydney Harbor |
| **i**sland | **r**ainforests | **z**inc is a mineral mined there |

# North-South-East-West
by Ethel Condon

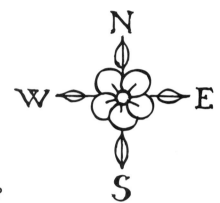

▶ **Materials:** N, S, E, W labeled in classroom

▶ **Here's How!**

Ask individuals or the whole class to respond to questions about the location of objects in the classroom. For example:

- What is on the north wall?
- The clock is in which direction?
- What rectangular shape is in the east?
- Who is sitting one person north of Brandon?
- In what direction are you facing if you look at the coat closet?
- If you are facing east and then turn to face south, which way did you turn?
- I am standing in the middle of the room. In what direction must I go to reach your desk?

▶ **Variations**

- When students are proficient in the four basic directions, add *northeast*, *northwest*, *southeast*, and *southwest*.

- Ask students to follow your directions to mentally move from place to place in the room. Step off several challenges in advance so you know that they are correct. (Remember to use a shorter stride.) For example:

  You are standing at the chalkboard. You walk five steps south, three steps east, and then two steps south again. Where are you?

# Who's There?

by Tekla White

▶ **Materials:** chart paper with names of animal habitats, colored marking pens

▶ **Here's How!**

1. In advance, write the names of various animal habitats on chart paper. (See examples below.)

2. Divide students into as many groups as the habitats listed. Give each group a different-colored marking pen. Groups choose one student to be the recorder.

3. Give a habitat chart to each group. Set a specific amount of time (2 minutes) for the groups to list animals found in that habitat.

4. At the end of the allotted time, instruct groups to pass their charts to another group. The second group evaluates the previous group's responses, writing a "?" by entries they feel are incorrect. They then add their own responses.

5. Repeat this process as time permits until as many groups as possible have worked on each habitat chart. Then post the charts and evaluate the responses as a class.

| Small Habitats | Large Habitats |
| --- | --- |
| in a tree | forest |
| under a rock | ocean |
| in a cave | rainforest |
| in a flower bed | desert |
| under a flowerpot | tundra |
| in a tide pool | city |
| on a rock at the shore | plains |
| in a puddle | pond |
| | river |
| | underground |
| | polar regions |
| | mountains |

polar

ocean

forest

fox
squirrel
owl
deer
skunk

# Around, and Around, and Around

by Tekla White

▶ **Materials:** string, a yardstick, meterstick, or ruler, a different set of round objects for each team (see box below), paper, pencils

▶ **Here's How!**

1. Divide students into teams of four or five.

2. Give each group a set of round objects, a yardstick or ruler, and lots of string.

3. Set up the activity by explaining that Professor Smart's space robot has been collecting round objects that were circling the earth. The professor wants to classify the objects by size. He's asking for your help. Here's what to do:

   - Measure the distance around each object. (Some teams may need to discuss how to measure the object, but when one team encircles an object with the string and measures the string with the ruler or yardstick, the other groups will see what to do.)

   - Record the name of each object and its measurement.

   - Arrange the objects in a line from smallest to largest.

4. If time permits, each group may share their results.

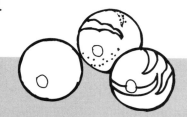

**Suggestions for Round Objects**
marbles
small rubber balls
small roundish rocks
walnuts
round fruits—apples, oranges, plums, melons, etc.
balls of modeling clay
larger balls—softballs, soccer balls, basketballs

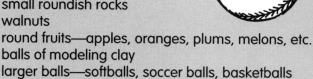

# Classy Classifications

### by Tekla White

▶ **Materials:** Venn diagram on chart paper for each group, a bag of assorted objects for each group (see box below), paper, pencils

▶ **Here's How!**

1. In advance, prepare a Venn diagram on large paper for each group. Label the diagram as shown.

2. Divide the class into groups of four or fewer.

3. Give each group a bag of assorted objects and a Venn diagram.

4. Groups classify the objects by placing them in the correct section of the diagram. Objects that are comprised of more than one material go in the section of the diagram that includes those materials.

5. Rotate groups so that they may check each other's classifications. If they see something out of place, they discuss the problem with the group who classified the objects.

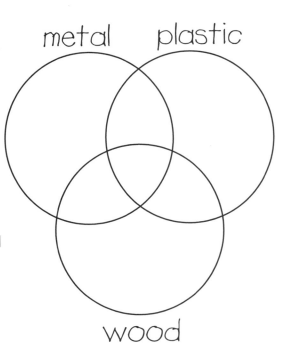

**Possible Objects to Sort**

Metal—paper clips, scissors, coins, flatware, binder clips, wire, nuts, bolts, screws, nails, wire hanger

Plastic—plastic utensils, "baggies," glue bottles, straws, coffee stirrers, cups, math manipulatives, plastic hanger

Wood—rulers, blocks, toothpicks, craft sticks

Mixed—scissors with plastic handles, wooden ruler with metal edge, pencil, wristwatch, wooden hanger with metal hook, writing pens, pushpins, tape dispensers, calculators

# Bird Brains

by Tekla White

▶ **Materials:** paper, pencils, reference books (optional)

▶ **Here's How!**

1. Depending on how you wish to conduct this activity, provide small groups or individuals with paper and pencils.

2. Challenge students to list as many birds as they can in a given amount of time. Provide several well-known examples to get them started (e.g., robin, seagull, parrot).

3. Compile the lists into categories such as:

Birds We See Here

Water Birds

Birds of Prey

Song Birds

Perching Birds

Wading Birds

Birds That Live in _____

### Examples of Birds

| | | | | | | | |
|---|---|---|---|---|---|---|---|
| albatross | blackbird | bluejay | bobwhite | cardinal | chickadee | chicken | crane |
| crow | eagle | dove | duck | falcon | finch | flamingo | hawk |
| heron | kiwi | macaw | magpie | oriole | ostrich | owl | wren |
| parakeet | partridge | peacock | pelican | penguin | pheasant | pigeon | puffin |
| quail | raven | sparrow | stork | swallow | swan | toucan | turkey |
| vulture | woodpecker | | hummingbird | | meadowlark | | |

# Why They Fly

by Delana Heidrich

▶ **Materials:** copy paper, model or picture of an airplane, chalkboard, chalk

▶ **Here's How!**

1. Cut paper lengthwise to create 1"-wide (2.5 cm) strips. Give each student one strip of paper.

2. Direct students to hold one end of the paper strip between their thumb and forefinger. Demonstrate how to hold the paper strip just below the lower lip.

3. Say, "I am going to blow on this paper. What do you think will happen?" List responses on the chalkboard and tally the number of students choosing each response.

4. Now direct students to blow on their paper strips. Rather than blowing the strips downward, students will notice that the strips rise.

5. Show a model or picture of an airplane. Ask if anyone can apply what just happened to explain how airplanes can fly. (Blowing on the top surface of the paper strip creates a low-pressure area which air below the strip tries to fill by rising. This is called Bernoulli's principle.)

▶ **Variation**

Conduct a paper airplane contest in which students try to construct planes of paper that will fly the farthest, highest, and/or straightest.

# Holey Hands!

by Delana Heidrich

▶ **Materials:** copy paper

▶ **Here's How!**

1. Distribute one sheet of paper to each student.

2. Students roll their papers vertically into long tubes.

3. Direct students to hold the tube up to one eye and close the other eye.

4. Place the free hand against the side of the tube with the palm facing the nose.

5. Open the closed eye. (Wait for giggles!) It should appear that there is a hole in the hand.

6. Explain that this is an *optical illusion.* It occurs because a person's two eyes are accustomed to meeting at a distant point to allow one to see in three dimensions. In this experiment, a person's two eyes cannot focus on the same view because the tube directs the right eye to see a distant scene, while the left eye is blocked from this view by the hand. The only way the brain can make sense of this is to put both images together, showing the object seen through the tube on the hand.

▶ **Variations**

- Have students decorate their tubes and present this experiment as a magic trick to younger students on the playground.

- Locate and share with your class other optical illusions. Many books on the subject are available.

# Motion Pictures

by Delana Heidrich

▶ **Materials:** unlined paper and pencils

▶ **Here's How!**

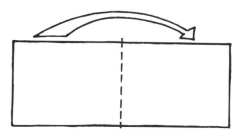

1. Provide each student with a piece of paper measuring about 10" x 4" (25.5 x 10 cm).

2. Direct each student to fold his or her paper in half crosswise to produce a 5" x 4" (13 x 10 cm) strip with the fold at the left.

3. Now, on the right end of the top layer, direct students to draw a picture of a man running.

4. Now draw a picture of a man standing still on the bottom layer of the paper, exactly beneath the picture of the man running.

5. Direct students to twist the top layer of the paper around a pencil. Then ask them to place the paper directly on their desks. Now students unroll the paper from their pencils and move their pencils back and forth over the top layer of the paper so that the bottom layer with the picture of the man standing still appears and disappears.

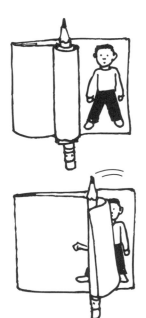

6. Explain that the eye retains the image of the still man even when it is presented with the image of the running man, so it puts the two pictures together to create the illusion of motion. The same thing happens in the production of cartoons. The images drawn to create a cartoon are still, but they appear to move when viewed at a rate of several slightly different still images per second.

# Note Card Inertia

by Delana Heidrich

▶ **Materials:** index cards, coffee cup, coin

▶ **Here's How!**

1. Place a 4" x 6" (10 x 15 cm) index card atop a coffee cup. Place a coin atop the card.

2. Tell students you are going to pull the card off the cup. Ask them to predict where the coin will go.

3. Quickly pull the card off the cup. Instead of flying along with the card, the coin will drop into the cup.

4. Explain to students that the coin dropped straight down due to the principle of *inertia*—a thing at rest has a tendency to stay at rest.

▶ **Variation**

Rather than snapping the card toward you to remove it from the cup, try flicking the card off the cup (and away from you) using your middle finger and thumb. This also results in the coin landing in the cup, and makes an impressive demonstration.

# Let's Do Lunch!

by Jodee Mueller & David Gerk

▶ **Materials:** food pyramid, school lunch menu, paper, pencils

▶ **Here's How!**

1. Divide students into pairs.

2. Students divide their papers into six sections and label each section according to the food pyramid.

   - fats, oils, and sweets
   - milk, yogurt, and cheese
   - meat, poultry, fish, dry beans, eggs, and nuts
   - vegetables
   - fruits
   - bread, cereal, rice, and pasta

3. Students look at the week's menu and write each food item in the correct section.

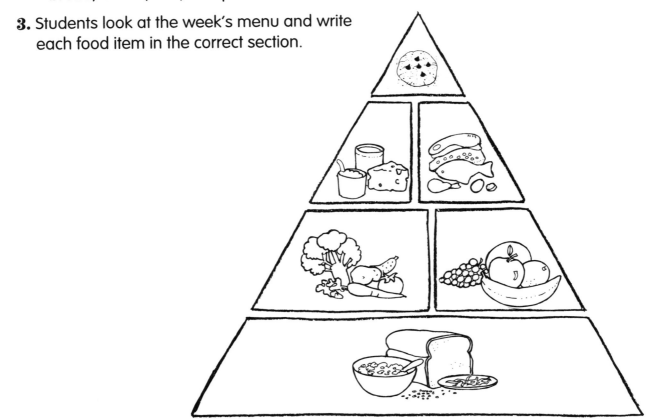

# Out of This World

by Jodee Mueller & David Gerk

▶ **Materials:** overhead projector, paper, pencils

▶ **Here's How!**

1. Prepare an overhead transparency giving the planet names in order. Underline the first letter of each planet.

2. Divide students into pairs or small groups.

3. Share the list of planets and the sentence. Discuss how the sentence helps to remember the names of the planets in order.

4. Direct students to write their own sentence. The first word of the sentence should begin with an *M* for *Mercury*, the second should begin with a *V* for *Venus*, etc.

<u>M</u>ercury
 <u>V</u>enus
  <u>E</u>arth
   <u>M</u>ars
    <u>J</u>upiter
     <u>S</u>aturn
      <u>U</u>ranus
       <u>N</u>eptune
        <u>P</u>luto

My very energetic mother just served us nine pizzas.

**Other Pneumonic Devices**

Colors of the rainbow—ROY G BIV (red, orange, yellow, green, blue, indigo, violet)
Scientific nomenclature—<u>K</u>ing <u>P</u>hillip <u>c</u>ame <u>o</u>ver for <u>G</u>ene's <u>s</u>pecial (kingdom, phylum, class, order, genus, species)

# You've Got the Beat

by Jodee Mueller & David Gerk

▶ **Materials:** paper, pencils, clock with a second hand

▶ **Here's How!**

1. Show students how to find their pulses. The easiest place is on the neck to the side of the windpipe.

2. When all students have located their pulse, have them count the beats for 15 seconds, beginning when you say "start" and ending when you say "stop."

3. Have students write down this number and multiply it by four. The resulting number is the resting heart rate for 1 minute.

4. Then time students as they run in place for 3 minutes. Determine the pulse rate in the same manner. The resulting number is the heart rate following exercise.

▶ **Variation**

Encourage students to do this on their own while they're still in bed in the morning, after getting ready for school, or after a meal.

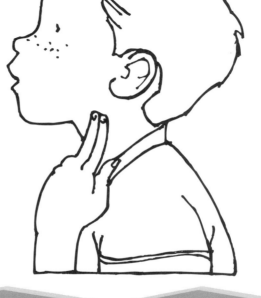

158

# Veggie Variety

by Jodee Mueller & David Gerk

▶ **Materials:** chalkboard, chalk, paper, pencils

▶ **Here's How!**

1. Share these riddles with students. Discuss the double meaning of some of the clues.

I'm edible.
I grow in a garden.
I'm rooted in your good health.
I'm orange and green.
What am I?
*(carrot)*

You throw away the outside.
Then you cook the inside.
Then you eat the outside and throw away the inside.
What am I?
*(corn on the cob)*

A bib is part of my wardrobe.
You see many icebergs when shopping for me.
I like to get dressed up.
I'm always a**head** of the rest of the meal.
What am I?
*(lettuce)*

I don't need glasses.
I spend most of my life in the dark.
I can speak French.
People fry, bake, and mash me!
What am I?
*(potato)*

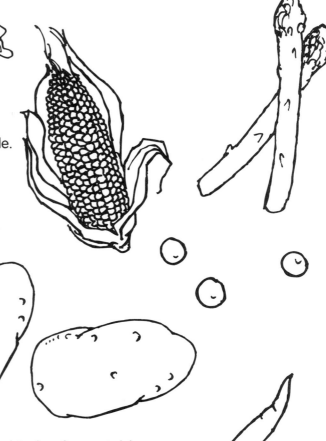

2. Brainstorm and list on the chalkboard other kinds of vegetables.

3. Divide students into small groups or pairs to write their own vegetable riddles.

4. During another 10-minute period, let students share their riddles.

# Animal Attraction

by Jodee Mueller & David Gerk

▶ **Materials:** chalkboard, colored chalk

▶ **Here's How!**

1. Draw five large boxes on the chalkboard. Label the boxes "Mammals," "Birds," "Reptiles," "Amphibians," and "Fish."

2. Divide students into groups. Assign each group a color.

3. Give the first group the name of an animal. (See charts below.) Ask in which classification the animal belongs.

4. If their answer is correct, write it in that box, using the color designated for that team. If the answer is not correct, ask the next group to place the same animal.

5. Continue until all animals have been placed in the correct family.

6. After all animals have been placed, award groups a point for every correct answer.

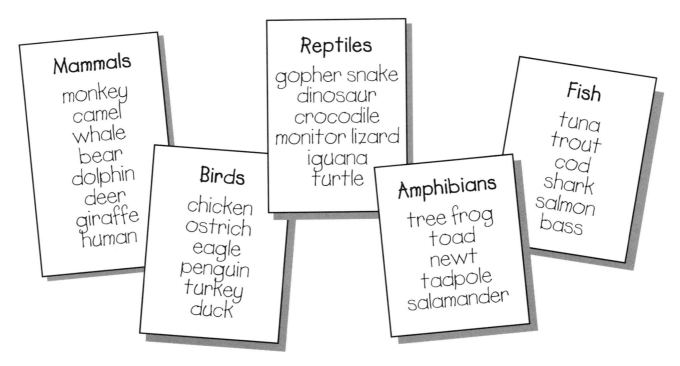

Mammals
monkey
camel
whale
bear
dolphin
deer
giraffe
human

Reptiles
gopher snake
dinosaur
crocodile
monitor lizard
iguana
turtle

Birds
chicken
ostrich
eagle
penguin
turkey
duck

Amphibians
tree frog
toad
newt
tadpole
salamander

Fish
tuna
trout
cod
shark
salmon
bass

# Let's Play Catch

by Jodee Mueller & David Gerk

▶ **Materials:** ruler, paper, pencils

▶ **Here's How!**

1. Explain to students that they are going to test their reaction times (how long it takes for the body to respond to a message sent to the brain by the senses).

2. Divide students into pairs.

3. One student lays his or her dominant arm on a table or desk with the hand over the edge. Space the thumb and index finger about 2" (5 cm) apart.

4. The partner holds the 12" (30 cm) end of the ruler, with the other end just above the other's open thumb and index finger.

5. The person holding the ruler says "now" and drops the ruler. The object is to catch the ruler between the thumb and forefinger as quickly as possible.

6. Read the distance by looking at the number on the ruler directly above the fingers.

7. Record the results. Repeat the procedure eight times.

8. Partners switch roles.

9. Compare the results as a class.

▶ **Variation**

Repeat the procedure using the nondominant hand. Compare the results.

# You Name It

by Martha Cheney

▶ **Materials:** chalkboard and chalk

▶ **Here's How!**

1. Choose the name of a student at random.

2. Write the letters in the name vertically on the chalkboard.

3. Next, choose a category that relates to some area of your science study. For example:

| Animals | Foods | Insects | Inventions |
| Plants | Colors | Flowers | Weather |
| Mammals | Space | Ocean Life | Rocks and Minerals |

4. Challenge students to find an item in the category that begins with each letter in the name. If a letter is repeated, a new item must be named.

5. Write the items next to the letters in the name.

▶ **Variation**

Across the top of the board, write two or more categories. For every letter in the student's name, the class must think of an item for each category.

R ockfish
E el
G ray whale
G rouper
I ntertidal zone
E chinoderm

# Is It Logical?
### by Martha Cheney

▶ **Materials:** overhead transparency with syllogisms

▶ **Here's How!**

1. In advance, write syllogisms on an overhead transparency. (See examples below.)

2. Explain to students that a *syllogism* gives **two premises**, which are assumed to be valid. These premises are **followed by a statement**. The syllogism is valid if the statement logically follows from the first two sentences, even if it is a silly idea or not true.

3. Show a syllogism. Students must use logic to determine if the statement is true or false.

**Examples of Syllogisms**

All elephants are mammals.
All mammals have hair.
Therefore, all elephants have hair. (Valid)

All horses eat grass.
Fred is a horse.
Therefore, Fred eats grass. (Valid)

All purkles are green.
Some green things are fuzzy.
Therefore, all purkles are fuzzy. (Not valid)

All zingdots are moldy.
Some moldy things are blue.
Therefore, all zingdots are blue. (Not valid)

All babies are cute.
No cute things cry.
Therefore, no babies cry. (Valid)

All politicians are smart.
All nice people are smart.
Therefore, all nice people are politicians. (Not valid)

All math is difficult.
No science is math.
Therefore, no science is difficult. (Not valid)

All frogs are green.
All green things are ugly.
Therefore, all frogs are ugly. (Valid)

# What If?

### by Martha Cheney

▶ **Materials:** none

▶ **Here's How!**

1. Propose a scenario that will allow students to apply their knowledge to new and problematic situations. Each scenario is called a "What if...?"

   - What if we came to school and our classroom was filled with Jell-O®?

   - What if scientists were able to clone a Tyrannosaurus Rex?

   - What if gravity disappeared for a day?

   - What if all the animals escaped from zoos and were loose in the cities?

   - What if you were suddenly an adult and your parents were children?

2. Give students time to reflect on the question. If students don't respond right away, allow some silent time for ideas to develop.

3. Challenge students to describe the effects of each scenario and to propose solutions to the problems they identify.

▶ **Variation**

Have students write their own "What if" scenarios on slips of paper for future consideration by the class.

# A Good Defense

by Jodee Mueller & David Gerk

▶ **Materials:** paper, pencils

▶ **Here's How!**

1. Divide students into groups.

2. Discuss ways animals protect themselves and examples of each.

   skunk (scent glands, terrible odor, etc.)        elk (antlers)

   porcupine (quills)                                chameleon (camouflage)

   armadillo (armor)                                 rattlesnake (poison)

   walrus (tusks)                                    gazelle (speed)

3. Tell students that they are going to write a description of the defense mechanisms of a newly discovered animal, the snarflebotter.

4. Allow 3 minutes or so for groups to write their descriptions, and then have a member of each group read their description to the class.

▶ **Variation**

During another 10-minute period, expand the description of the snarflebotter to include its habitat, diet, etc.

# Rock Out

### by Jill Norris

▶ **Materials:** five rocks, index cards, paper, pencils

▶ **Here's How!**

1. In advance, gather five distinctive rocks. These should be large enough to be viewed from any seat in the classroom. Fold and number an index card to designate each rock.

2. Line the rocks up at the front of the classroom

3. Give students 3 minutes to write a description of one rock.

4. Individuals read their descriptions, and then classmates give the number of the rock being described.

▶ **Variation**

List characteristics of rocks (smooth, lumpy, rough, pointed, rounded, multicolored, etc.). Write the numbers of the displayed rocks having each characteristic.

# Them Bones

by Marilyn Evans

▶ **Materials:** chart paper, marking pens

▶ **Here's How!**

1. Divide students into small groups. Give each group a piece of chart paper and a marking pen.

2. Groups choose a recorder and write their group number (or recorder's name) on the paper.

3. Give groups up to 5 minutes to record the names of bones in the human body. They may use either the common or scientific name. Common names (e.g., kneecap, collarbone) are worth 1 point each; scientific names (i.e., patella, scapula) are worth 2 points each.

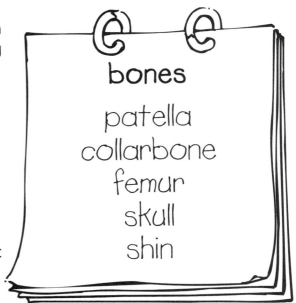

bones

patella
collarbone
femur
skull
shin

4. Collect and post all the charts.

5. As a class, read each group's list and assign points to correct responses.

▶ **Variation**

Post the lists of bones generated in the original activity. Challenge groups to group the bones by body parts (e.g., leg bones, arm bones, bones in the thorax, etc.), and then create a song or chant to relate the names.

# Simple Machines Hunt

by Jill Norris

▶ **Materials:** chalkboard, chalk, scissors, hole punch

▶ **Here's How!**

1. Draw a large Venn diagram on the chalkboard as shown.

2. Ask students to think of other simple machines and tell in which section of the diagram the objects should be written. If students have difficulty, name some simple machines for them. Point out that some tools may be a combination of simple machines and that those would go in the intersecting sections of the diagram.

lever    wedge

nail clippers
screwdriver
seesaw
doorstop
can opener
tape dispenser
rolling pin   top
bicycle wheels
doorknob

wheel & axle

3. Hold up the scissors. Ask questions to help students decide in which section of the diagram scissors belong. Repeat with the hole punch (between lever and wedge).

# What Will It Need?

by Jill Norris

▶ **Materials:** paper, pencils, chalkboard, chalk, chart paper

▶ **Here's How!**

1. Divide students into small groups.

2. Write a habitat on the chalkboard.

| | |
|---|---|
| desert | mountain |
| ocean | river |
| pond | swamp |
| polar | rainforest |
| temperate forest | |

3. Direct groups to brainstorm and list the characteristics that an animal would be likely to have to survive in that habitat. (See examples below.)

4. Compile the groups' responses into a single chart.

pond

polar

desert

withstand heat; get water from food; body coloring in earth tones

**Examples of Habitats and Animal Characteristics**

desert—able to withstand heat, able to get water from food, body covering in earth tones
polar—thick body covering and/or fat layer, may be white, likely to need to swim to get food, likely to eat fish

# Think Fast

by Marilyn Evans

▶ **Materials:** none

▶ **Here's How!**

1. As a class, agree upon three categories from your science studies. For example, space, weather, and invertebrates.

2. The class stands in a circle. A student chosen to be IT stands in the center of the circle.

3. IT points to anyone and names one of the three categories. *(Weather!)*

4. The student pointed to has 3 seconds to name something related to weather. *(Tornado!)* If the student answers incorrectly or does not respond within the time allotted, he or she becomes IT.

5. IT continues to point to students in the circle and call out one of the three categories. The same category or person may be called several times in succession.

▶ **Variation**

IT names a category and points at one student. That student gives a word in the category, the student to his or her immediate right gives a word, and so on until there is an incorrect answer or no response. Then IT points to a new student and names another category.

Weather!

# Horsefeathers
by Marilyn Evans

▶ **Materials:** lists of science facts

▶ **Here's How!**

1. In advance, prepare several lists of statements about topics the class has studied in science. (Although you could be extemporaneous, the fun of the game depends on a rapid succession of statements.)

2. Explain to students that the expression "Horsefeathers!" means that something is ridiculously untrue. Inform them that you are going to rapidly relate science information, but that at some point you will say something untrue. When they hear that statement, they are to shout, "Horsefeathers!"

**A game of Horsefeathers might proceed like this:**
Fish have fins.
Fish breathe with gills.
A fish will die out of water.
A group of fish is called a school.
A whale is a fish.
*Horsefeathers!*
Electricity is a form of energy.
Electricity is created by moving electrons.
Electricity is a solid.
*Horsefeathers!*

▶ **Variation**

After students have played this game a few times, challenge them to create prompts for the game.

# It's Not Possible!
by Susan Kunze

▶ **Materials:** straight-backed chairs, small objects to pick up

▶ **Here's How!**

1. **Impossible Task 1**—Have students sit back in chairs with their feet together on the floor and arms folded. Ask them to try to stand up without leaning forward or using their arms or hands. The force of gravity will keep them in their chairs, because their legs aren't directly under their centers of gravity and can't create enough force to push them up.

2. **Impossible Task 2**—Have students stand with the right side of their body and right foot directly against a wall and then try to raise their left foot and keep it up.

3. **Impossible Task 3**—Have students stand with their back, from head to heels, pressed against the wall. Place a small object (an eraser, a piece of candy, etc.) approximately 12" in front of their feet, and then challenge them to pick it up without bending their knees or moving their heels from the wall.

4. Now that students are dumbfounded, explain why they were not able to complete these simple tasks:

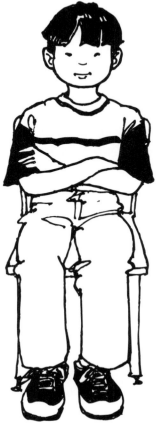

> Our center of gravity is in our torso, with our weight evenly balanced around it.

> Anytime we want to move, our muscles must overcome the force of gravity pulling on our center. Students were not able to do the movements requested because the position of the center of gravity in each one makes it difficult for our muscles to create enough force to overcome it.

# Know Your Neighbor

by Delana Heidrich

▶ **Materials:** paper, pencils

▶ **Here's How!**

1. Divide the class into two teams.

2. Each student writes a response to a close-ended-opinion question you ask of the entire group (e.g., "Would you rather spend a week in Paris or at Disneyland?").

3. Choose someone from Team 1 to be IT. IT tries to prove he or she knows his or her neighbors by identifying one person from Team 2 who answered the question in the same way.

4. Both students read their responses aloud. If their responses match, Team 1 receives a point. If their responses do not match, neither team receives a point.

5. Choose a student from Team 2 to attempt to "know your neighbor."

6. Continue play until all class members have had a chance to be IT.

**Sample Questions**
1. Would you like to spend your entire life being 18 years old?
2. Would you like to have greater or fewer than two children when you grow up?
3. Tell the truth: Do you miss going to school just a little bit during the summer months?
4. Which of the following school subjects do you like the most: math, science, English?
5. Do you ever hope to become famous?

# Humming Hounds
by Laurie Williams

▶ **Materials:** classroom objects

▶ **Here's How!**

1. One student leaves the classroom.

2. Choose an object such as a ball, pen, or mitten to hide in the classroom.

3. When the student returns, the class begins to hum softly, getting louder as the student gets closer to the object.

4. The student doesn't know what object he or she is looking for. The humming is the clue that he or she is close or far away.

5. Students clap when the student has picked up the correct object.

▶ **Variations**

Use sounds other than humming to signal the seeker:

- snap fingers slowly at first and then snap faster as the student gets closer
- whistle quietly, then louder
- tap feet slowly, then faster

# Shoe Salad

by Laurie Williams

▶ **Materials:** students' shoes, timer

▶ **Here's How!**

1. All students take off their shoes and put them in a huge pile in the center of the classroom.

2. Choose one student to try to match each pair of shoes to its owner. Set a timer for 3 minutes.

3. The student who is doing the matching lays each pair of shoes by the student he or she thinks they belong to, but no one puts their shoes back on.

4. When the timer goes off, everyone with the correct pair of shoes in front of them raises their hands.

5. The student scores as many points as there are correctly matched shoes.

6. Put the shoes back in the pile and give another student a chance at matching them to their owners.

# Amazing Memory
by Laurie Williams

▶ **Materials:** various classroom articles, paper, pencils

▶ **Here's How!**

1. Put up to 25 objects on a tray or classroom desk and cover them up. Place the tray or desk in a place where students can gather around and view the items.

> **Examples of Items**
> rubber band, stapler, Post-it® note, pencil, paper clip, thumbtack, ruler, eraser, mouse pad, pen, crayon, marker, glue stick, textbook, hole punch, sticker, candy, envelope, masking tape, protractor, computer disk

2. Invite all students at the same time to come to the desk and study the items for exactly 1 minute.

3. Students return to their seats and write down as many items as they can remember.

4. Have partners check each other's lists and record a score for the number of objects correctly named.

5. Discuss any strategies that students used to help themselves remember the items.

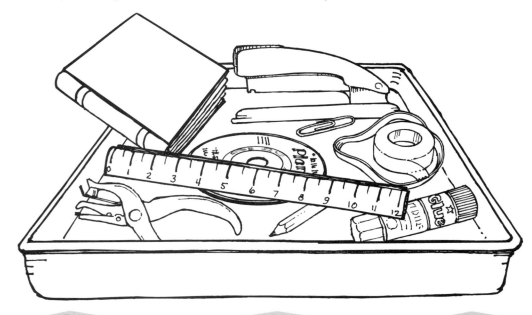

# Skittish

by Laurie Williams

▶ **Materials:** skit prompts on pieces of paper

▶ **Here's How!**

1. In advance, prepare a silly skit prompt using the same three words for each group—a person (or animal), a place, and a thing. (See examples in the box below.)

2. Divide students into groups of four or five.

3. Give the groups 5 minutes to make up a skit to perform that incorporates all three nouns written on the prompt. For example:

> Each group is given a piece of paper with the words *Sally Ride* (person), *swimming pool* (place), and *snorkel* (thing). They might make up a skit about Sally Ride completing her mission in space, and then relaxing at a swimming pool, learning to snorkel.

4. Let each group perform their skit for the others.

---

**Possible Skit Prompts**

Sally Ride, swimming pool, snorkel      cowboy, airport, suitcase
bear, grocery store, watermelon      kangaroo, school, swings

---

▶ **Variations**

- Give each group different prompts, and have the audience guess what the person, place, and thing are. The performers cannot say the words that the audience is to guess, but they must be clever in their acting to give clues and hints.

  For example: Given Sally Ride, a swimming pool, and a snorkel, the group might act out swimming and snorkeling and address the person portraying Sally Ride by saying, "Wow, how does it feel to be the first woman in space? Now, you can take up a new hobby and learn to identify underwater animals and plant life with a mask and J-shaped pipe that fits into your mouth to breathe underwater."

- Each group makes up a prompt. Groups switch prompts and develop their skits.

# Going on a Field Trip

by Laurie Williams

▶ **Materials:** none

▶ **Here's How!**

1. Students sit with you in a circle on the floor so that all students can see each other.

2. Begin by saying, "I'm going on a field trip and I'm bringing a school bus."

3. The next student says, "I'm going on a field trip and I'm bringing a school bus and a sack lunch" (or another original idea).

4. Continue around the circle with each student attempting to recall, in order, what has previously been said.

5. When a student is unable to remember all the items, her or she may begin the game again with, "I'm going on a field trip and I'm bringing a school bus."

▶ **Variation**

Students say only things that begin with the letter of their first name. For example, a student named **R**eagan would say, "I'm bringing **r**aisins," and a student named **G**lenn would say, "I'm bringing my **g**lasses."

# Rainy Day Walk

by Tekla White

▶ **Materials:** music with a moderate beat

▶ **Here's How!**

1. Demonstrate the following feet and hand movements without music:

   - Begin with feet slightly apart.
   - Step (sideways) on the right foot. Tap left toe by right foot.
   - Step (sideways) on the left foot. Tap right toe by left foot.
   - Walk forward four steps. Bend arms at the elbow (palms face forward) on step one, hands at sides on step two.
   - Repeat with steps 3 and 4.
   - Repeat the sequence until the music ends.

2. Have the students practice the movements.

3. Play the music of your choice and have the class imitate the motions with the music.

▶ **Variation**

Divide students into groups and ask each group to invent a series of four to eight hand and feet movements. Groups teach their movements to the class.

# Water, Water, Everywhere

by Tekla White

▶ **Materials for each team:** two plastic water containers, two towels, extra towel or mop

▶ **Here's How!**

1. Prepare for this relay race by placing a container on a towel at each end of the course.

2. Put the same amount of water in each container at one end of the course.

3. Divide students into teams and have them line up behind the container with water in it.

4. The first student carries (speed walking only) the full container to the empty one and pours the water into the empty container. She or he returns to the line with the empty container.

5. The next student in line takes the empty container and speed walks to the full container. He or she fills the empty container and then carries it back to the line.

6. The relay continues until everyone in the line has had a turn.

7. The team with the most water in the container at the end of the relay is the winner.

# Jug Toss

by Tekla White

▶ **Materials:** one plastic gallon jug for each student, scissors, a beanbag for every two students

▶ **Here's How!**

1. To prepare for the game, cut the bottom half off the jugs, leaving the handle in place.

2. Two students stand a few feet from each other.

3. Holding the jug by the handle, students toss and catch the beanbags with their jugs.

4. Each time they successfully toss and catch the bag, they move one step farther from each other.

▶ **Variation**

The whole class can play the game together. After each toss, the pairs who failed to catch the beanbag sit down. The last pair standing is the winner.

# Zoo Break
by Tekla White

▶ **Materials:** two small stuffed animals or beanbags

▶ **Here's How!**

1. The playing area can be the entire classroom. Any area, however, can be declared out-of-bounds or unsafe.

2. One student is the zoo keeper. The zoo keeper is the only person who can walk or run.

3. All the students are trees. They cannot move their feet (roots). Trees may stand in a circle, in lines, or in random positions around the room.

4. Two of the trees are given beanbags or stuffed animals.

5. The trees toss the animals from one tree to another.

6. The zoo keeper tries to stop the zoo break by intercepting the animals in the air or on the ground or by tagging a tree holding an animal. If an animal falls on the floor, trees can bend to pick it up, but they can't move their roots. If a tree moves its roots, the keeper gains the animal.

7. When both animals have been captured, the zoo keeper appoints a new keeper and throws the animals to trees who have not yet thrown the animals.

8. Trees may stretch and change places before the game begins again.

▶ **Variations**

• Increase the number of toy animals or beanbags and appoint two zoo keepers.

• Trees form two lines, one on each side of the room facing each other. One or more keepers are stationed between the lines. They try to catch the animals as they are thrown.

# An Eggstra Silly Relay

by Tekla White

▶ **Materials:** plastic spoon for each student, plastic egg for each team

▶ **Here's How!**

1. Divide the class into teams.

2. Designate a course around or across the room. This may involve going around objects or it can be a straight line.

3. The first team member navigates the course carrying a plastic egg in a spoon. If the egg drops, the person must replace the egg, take five steps backward, and then continue.

4. Upon returning to the team, the student transfers the egg (hands don't touch the egg) to the spoon of the next student in line.

5. The first team to have all members complete the course is the winner.

# Follow the Leaders

by Tekla White

▶ **Materials:** none

▶ **Here's How**

1. Divide students into pairs.

2. Allow 3 minutes for pairs to create and practice a routine of five different movements.

3. Choose a pair to demonstrate their routine to the class.

4. Class members attempt to copy the routine.

5. Choose a new pair to demonstrate their routine and continue the game.

# Who's Missing?
by Marilyn Evans

▶ **Materials:** none

▶ **Here's How!**

1. Choose one student to be IT. IT closes his or her eyes.

2. Silently choose another student to leave the classroom or to hide out of sight.

3. The remaining students change seats with one another.

4. When all students are in place, IT uncovers his or her eyes and tries to determine who has left the classroom.

5. Choose a new IT and repeat the game.

# Eagle Eyes

by Marilyn Evans

▶ **Materials:** none

▶ **Here's How!**

1. Choose one student to be the subject.

2. The subject stands in front of the class. Class members are directed to observe the subject very closely, noting as many details about the person's appearance and dress as possible.

3. The subject steps outside the classroom or goes to an area out of sight and changes **one** thing about himself or herself. For example:

   • remove a piece of jewelry or clothing
   • add a piece of jewelry or clothing
   • put hair behind one ear or change part of hair
   • roll up one pants leg
   • untie a shoe
   • put a pencil behind one ear
   • hook something under a belt
   • unbutton a shirt sleeve
   • turn a collar up or down

4. The subject returns to the front of the room.

5. Students attempt to determine the one aspect that has changed.

# Wheel of Fortune

### by Jill Norris

▶ **Materials:** chalkboard, chalk, game spinner

▶ **Here's How!**

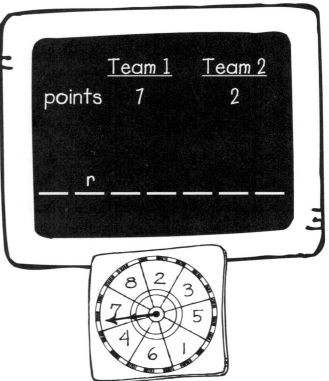

1. Divide the class into three or four teams. Each team needs to be seated together.

2. Draw a scoreboard on the chalkboard.

3. Draw blanks on the board to indicate each letter of a word or phrase from some area of study. For example:

   > product
   > tadpoles breathe with gills
   > Lewis and Clark
   > numerator and denominator
   > President _____
   > oxygen is a gas

4. Tell the class the category of the word or phrase. For example, a person, math words, science fact, etc.

5. The first member of Team 1 spins the spinner and calls out a letter. If that letter occurs in the puzzle, write it on the appropriate blank. Award the team the number of points indicated on the spinner for each time the letter occurs. For example: the spinner lands on 4, the student calls an "s," and there are two "s's"—Team 1 receives 8 points. Record all letters called on the board.

6. If the first member of the team called a correct letter, then the next member of that team gets to call a letter. A team continues to call out letters until there is an incorrect choice. Encourage the team members to collaborate on letter choices and to confer when a member thinks he or she knows the answer.

7. The team that solves the puzzle receives 10 additional points.

# The Paper Chase

by Marilyn Evans

▶ **Materials:** lots of scrap paper, ruler, yardstick, or meterstick

▶ **Here's How!**

1. In advance, cut paper into strips of equal width, but of varying lengths from 2" (5 cm) to 18" (45.5 cm), or longer if you have paper of longer lengths. Hide the paper strips around the room.

2. Divide students into three or four groups.

3. Explain that you have hidden lots of paper strips around the room; some are short, some are long.

4. Allow 3 minutes for the groups to find as many strips as possible.

5. Designate an area for each group to lay out their strips end to end.

6. Measure the lines of strips. The group with the longest line is the winner.

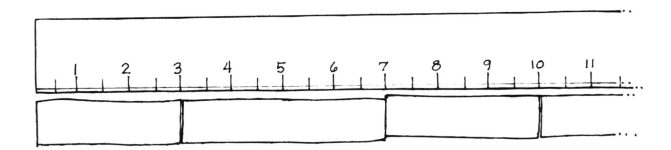

# One-Step-at-a-Time Relay

by Jo Ellen Moore

▶ **Materials:** construction paper

▶ **Here's How!**

1. Divide students into teams of no more than six.

2. Give each team two pieces of construction paper large enough for one member to stand on.

3. Pick a starting and ending point in the room. (As this relay proceeds more slowly than most, limit the distance students need to move.)

4. The first player on each team puts down a paper, steps on it, puts down the other paper and steps on that one, picks up the first paper and puts it down farther ahead, and so on until the goal is reached. The player repeats the process back to the starting line.

5. The first player hands the two papers to the next player in line, who continues in the same manner.

6. The first team to finish is the winner.

# In the Zone

by Jill Norris

▶ **Materials:** Nerf® ball, wastebasket or large box

▶ **Here's How!**

1. Place a wastebasket or large box (the "basket") on a desk or table in the center of the room.

2. Students are to remain in their seats. Move students within six feet of the basket to another position.

3. Throw the Nerf® ball to any student and begin timing for 45 seconds.

4. Within the time limit, the ball must be tossed or passed to all students. The last student to get the ball shoots for the basket.

5. Award the class 1 point for every second under the time limit and 2 points if the basket was made.

6. Play more rounds as time allows.

You might set a goal for total points at the end of the playing session and offer a prize to the whole class if the goal is reached—extra recess minutes, free time, stickers, a small treat, etc.

# Red Hot Chili Peppers

by Marilyn Evans

▶ **Materials:** a ball or balloon

▶ **Here's How!**

1. Students form a circle, either sitting or standing.

2. Choose one student to be the Caller. The Caller stands outside the circle.

3. Whisper a "secret" number between 1 and 50 to the Caller.

4. The players in the circle move the ball from person to person around the circle. At the same time, the Caller counts aloud. When the Caller gets to the secret number, she or he shouts, "Red hot chili peppers!"

5. The player with the ball (or about to get the ball if it is in the air) must sit down in the center of the circle.

6. Choose a new Caller, whisper a new secret number, and begin play again.

7. Continue until only two players remain. The last person left without the ball when "Red hot chili peppers!" is called is the winner.

# Build a Sentence Relay

by Marilyn Evans

▶ **Materials:** words on index cards, chalkboard, chalk

▶ **Here's How!**

1. In advance, prepare a set of index cards, each containing a word that could start a sentence.

| The | During | Every | When | If |
|-----|--------|-------|------|-----|
| Some | A | That | I | One |
| Many | Each | An | As | After |

2. Divide the class into three teams, numbered 1 through 3.

3. Divide the chalkboard into three sections labeled with the team numbers.

4. The first member of each team draws a word card.

5. On command, the first team member races toward the board and writes the word from the card to begin the team's sentence.

6. The first player runs back to his or her team and hands the chalk to the next player. The second player runs to the board and writes the next word of his or her choice in the sentence, and so on.

7. The first team to write a full sentence in which all players have written at least one word is the winner. (All words must be spelled correctly.) If all team members have written a word but the sentence is not complete, players go again in order until the sentence is complete.